Anonymous

Spring Meeting, 1890

Anonymous

Spring Meeting, 1890

ISBN/EAN: 9783337377335

Printed in Europe, USA, Canada, Australia, Japan

Cover: Foto ©ninafisch / pixelio.de

More available books at **www.hansebooks.com**

NEW YORK ══════

══ ═══JOCKEY CLUB

MORRIS PARK

WEST CHESTER, N.Y.

SPRING MEETING, 1890

ADDED MONEY, $104,250

Races promptly at 2.30 P.M.

———◆———

T. H. KOCK   **H. DeCOURCY FORBES**

Secretary   President

OFFICES: 5TH AVENUE AND 22D STREET, NEW YORK

Morris Park.

HE LINES OF MORRIS PARK ARE ADMIrable. In every direction the eye is met by the graceful sweep of smooth, broad tracks and an endless stretch of close-cropped and velvety lawn. The stately vistas are shaded by bits of wood, and from the Club-House tower the glint of the rolling waters of the Sound can be seen. There is an extent and vastness about it that appeals to the mind and eye alike.

HE CLUB-HOUSE WILL BE UNIQUE. THE New York Jockey Club has a more diversified membership than any other organization on earth. It serves as the meeting-place for the more notable clubmen of a nation of sixty-five millions of people. There is now not a city in North America, of importance, whose representative clubmen are not enrolled to a greater or less number under the banner of the New York Jockey Club. During the race-meetings the Club-House will be the home of the most popular and important body of men in the country. All good Americans come to New York; once here they attend the races, and Morris Park is the rendezvous, as a matter of course.

THE RULE ADOPTED BY THE EXECUTIVE
Committee, making the members of all recognized Clubs
eligible for election to the New York Jockey Club, without
initiation fee, and for the small annual dues of $25 for
Resident Members, and $15 for Non-resident Members (over
90 miles from New York City), has been eagerly embraced.
The original motive of the founder of Morris Park, in
devoting such an unusual amount of luxury and convenience
to the Club-House, was to make special provision for clubmen living at a distance, who visited New York. Every
detail of the Club-House will be in keeping with modern
ideas of comfort and decoration, from the handsome ball-room,
dining-rooms, and bed-rooms to the elaborate baths and bowl-
ing-alleys in the basement. The fixtures for the coming
twelve months show that the Club-House will be occupied
all the year round, as there will be a succession of Baseball,
Lacrosse, Lawn Tennis, Athletic Games, Bicyciing, Football,
Cricket, and Polo matches. Special grounds have been laid
out for these sports, and the eight-mile cross-country track
has been fixed upon as the standard course for championship
cross-country running. The half-a-mile cinder path, twenty-
five feet wide, will undoubtedly be the common ground for
deciding high-class running contests. There has never here-
tofore been an accepted neutral ground for the more important
athletic struggles, and the rivalry of the big athletic clubs is
so bitter that sport has sometimes suffered thereby. All
classes of athletes have now fixed upon Morris Park. As the
athletic tracks and grounds are all "in field," and some
distance from the big stand, a portable grand stand accom-

grand Stand

modating five thousand people has been constructed, which can be placed at the point of greatest interest.

THE COMPLETION OF THESE ARRANGEMENTS will have an effect on the stamina and pluck of American athletes which it is difficult to exaggerate, for they will now have a championship course of unrivalled beauty, which will accommodate the largest possible crowds, and bring out large fields of contestants.

FOR HORSE RACING, PURE AND SIMPLE, there are three complete tracks: the famous three-quarter mile straight, on which the celebrated El Rio Rey ran three-quarters of a mile in 1.11; the mile-and-a-quarter track with one turn; and the mile-and-a-half track with two turns. The home stretch — 2,450 feet long and 100 feet broad through its whole length — is one of the finest in the world.

THE BEAUTY OF THE BUILDINGS IN THE Park, the symmetry of the landscape plan, and the splendor of color, which the gardeners and architects have given it, make a scene of unsurpassed attractiveness. The charm of the place is found mainly in the exquisite harmony between nature and art. There is literally not a bit of color on any of the buildings that dot the Park, which has not been the subject of exhaustive study and consideration. The whole landscape is graceful and comforting to the eye.

THE FREE FIELD, WHICH IS OPEN TO THE public without any charge whatever, is one of the special features. The Grand Stand, with the Betting Ring in the basement and a spacious promenade on the main floor, is a magnificent structure of brick and iron, 650 feet long and 150 feet deep, having a seating capacity of 10,000 people. In front of it a beautiful lawn slopes down to the track. The general attractions of the grounds are increased by the great array of stables, the trainers' club-house, and the picturesque cottages of the superintendent and other officials. The quarters of the Coaching Club, with a special house, are gracefully laid out, and the various bits of woodland have been prepared for picnic parties.

CRITICISM IS NEARLY ALWAYS COMPARATIVE. There are many famous race-courses in the world, and it is natural enough that Morris Park should be considered with them. Ascot has the stamp of royal patronage, and a superb approach through Windsor Park, but the buildings are antiquated and the enclosures cramped. The Derby is run on a course that is in no sense picturesque; and though Goodwood has many beautiful points, it does not boast supremacy. So, too, in France, Longchamps — the most famous, but not the best course — has an equipment in track buildings that seem meagre to Americans after the superb structures here. In Austria and Germany the tracks, in a general way, are small, with cosy but not pretentious quarters; while in Australia there are some good stretches of track, but no advance in modern scientific methods in the drainage or the buildings.

THE ALL-ROUND EQUIPMENT OF MORRIS Park is what has made its fame. It is within good driving distance of the first city of the country, near enough to the sea to get the salt breeze on the warmest days, and nestled in the heart of a bit of beautiful, rolling, fertile country.

IT WILL BE THE ENDEAVOR OF THE NEW York Jockey Club to make Morris Park, in all its details, the most attractive sporting centre of this continent. There is no form of reputable and popular sport which will not find a home on its grounds. They will never be closed. THE CLUB-HOUSE WILL BE AS COMFORTABLE in mid-winter as in the height of the season, and it will be kept up, in all respects, to the standard of the best city clubs.

RACE DAYS.

———

FRIDAY, MAY 30th. (Decoration Day.)	SATURDAY, JUNE 7th.
SATURDAY, MAY 31st.	TUESDAY, JUNE 10th.
TUESDAY, JUNE 3d.	WEDNESDAY, JUNE 11th.
WEDNESDAY, JUNE 4th.	THURSDAY, JUNE 12th.
THURSDAY, JUNE 5th.	FRIDAY, JUNE 13th.
FRIDAY, JUNE 6th.	SATURDAY, JUNE 14th.

The Grand Stand.

STAKES.

Date.	Race.	Distance.	Added Money.	No. Entries.
Friday, May 30th, (Decoration Day).	Galliard Stakes · · ·	½ m.	$1,500	138
	Withers Stakes · · ·	1 m.	2,000	139
	N.Y.J.C. Handicap ·	1¼ m.	5,000	68
Saturday, May 31st · ·	Debutante Stakes ·	⅝ m.	1,250	117
	Toboggan Slide Handicap · · · · ·	¾ m.	10,000	119
Tuesday, June 3d · · · ·	Van Nest Stakes · ·	⅝ m.	1,250	101
	Ladies' Stakes · · ·	1,400 yds.	1;500	99
Wednesday, June 4th · · ·	Juvenile Stakes · · ·	½ m.	1,500	63
	Fleetwood Stakes ·	1 m.	2,000	74
Thursday, June 5th · · ·	Casanova Stakes · ·	¾ m.	2,000	92
	Elms Stakes · · · ·	1⅛ m.	2,000	47
Saturday, June 7th · · ·	Bowling Brook Handicap · · · · ·	1⅛ m.	2,000	85
	All Breeze Stakes ·	⅞ m.	1,250	73
Tuesday, June 10th · ·	Larchmont Stakes ·	¾ m.	1,500	110
	Belmont Stakes · · ·	1¼ m.	3,000	136
Wednesday, June 11th · ·	Baychester Stakes ·	1 m.	1,250	87
	Fort Schuyler Stakes	1 m.	1,250	53
Thursday, June 12th · ·	Anticipation Stakes,	¾ m.	2,000	106
	Trial Stakes · · · · ·	1¼ m.	3,000	55
Saturday, June 14th · ·	Throgg's Neck Stakes · · · · · · ·	⅞ m.	1,250	60
	Great Eclipse Stakes	¾ m.	10,000	223
	West Chester Cup ·	1½ m.	3,000	34

New York Jockey Club.

SPRING MEETING.
1890.

FIRST DAY.—FRIDAY, MAY 30TH.
(DECORATION DAY.)

FIRST RACE. — Opening Scramble, for all ages. A sweepstakes of $15 each, with $750 added, of which $100 to second, and $50 to third. **Five Furlongs.**

SECOND RACE. — GALLIARD STAKES, for two years old. A sweepstakes of $50 each, h.f., or only $10 if declared by April 1st, with $1,500 added, of which $300 to second, and $200 to third. Closed January 2d, 1890, with 138 entries. **Half a Mile.**

1 Aby, C. W., ch. c. **Rodman,** Rutherford, Leveret.
2 Auburndale Stable, b. c. **Duke John,** Duke of Montrose, Reina Victoria.
3 Auburndale Stable, ch. f. ———, Onondaga, Gleam.
4 Barbee, Geo., br. c. **Druse,** Faustus, Drucilla.
5 Belmont, August, ch. c. **St. Charles,** St. Blaise, Carita.
6 Belmont, August, b. c. **Lepanto,** Kingfisher, Leightonia.
7 Belmont, August, blk. g. **Adair,** St. Blaise, Adosinda.
8 Belmont, August, ch. f. **La Tosca,** St. Blaise, Toucques.
9 Belmont, August, ch. f. **Flavia,** St. Blaise, Flavina.
10 Belmont, August, ch. f. **Beauty,** St. Blaise, Bella.
11 Belmont, August, ch. c. **Jack of Diamonds,** St. Blaise, Nellie James.
12 Belmont, August, ch. g. **St. Patrick,** St. Blaise, Patience.
13 Beverwyck Stable, b. f. **Lottie,** Faustus, Loretto.
14 Beverwyck Stable, ch. c. **Brocker,** Faustus, Lulu.
15 Beverwyck Stable, b. f. **Come and Go,** Alarm, Heel and Toe.
16 Beverwyck Stable, b. f. **Polly S.,** Pizarro, Amandine.
17 Beverwyck Stable, b. f. **Bertha Campbell,** King Alfonso, Vulpine.
18 Bonchurch Stable, b. c. **War Duke,** Duke of Montrose, Warover.
19 Brown, S. S., ch. c. ———, Richmond, Gladys.
20 Brown, S. S., ch. c. ———, Richmond, Mayfield.
21 Brown, S. S., ch. f. ———, Himyar, Jewel.
22 Bruce, L. C. ch. c. **Brentano,** Great Tom, Addie Hart.
23 Bruce, L. C., b. f. **Krikina,** Muscovy, Krik.
24 Castle Stable, b. c. **Glaucus,** Glenelg, La Polka.
25 Castle Stable, ch. f. **Thorndale,** Eolus, Lizzie Hazlewood.
26 Castle Stable, ch. c. **Glideaway,** Glenelg, Schott.
27 Conner, Wm. M., ch. f. **Furlano,** Woodlands, Waltz.
28 Conner, Wm. M., ch. f. **Gardelia,** Woodlands, Glidelia.
29 Corrigan, E., br. f. **Corine Buckingham,** Powhattan, Hattie Harris.
30 Cotton, J., ch. c. ———, Pontiac, Lizzie Mack.

31 Daly, John, ch. f. ———, Joe Daniels, Mottle.
32 Daly, Marcus, ch. c. **Gold Dollar**, Sir Modred, Trade Dollar.
33 Daly, Marcus, ch. f. **Leonora**, Sir Modred, Lizzie Lucas.
34 Daly, Marcus, b. f. **Mistletoe**, Sir Modred, Letola.
35 Daly, Marcus, b. c. **Montana**, Ban Fox, Queen.
36 Daly, Marcus, b. f. **Namouna**, Sir Modred, La Favorita.
37 Daly, Marcus, b. c. **Prince Charming**, Sir Modred, Carissima.
38 Daly, Marcus, ch. c. **Silver King**, St. Blaise, Maud Hampton.
39 Daly, W. C., b. f. **Kate Clark**, St. Blaise, Felicia.
40 Davis & Hall, ch. c. **Keyser**, Luke Blackburn, Janet Norton.
41 Davis & Hall, br. c. **Grafton**, Gaberlunzie, Olive Branch.
42 Davis & Hall, b. f. **Gaiety**, Gaberlunzie, Kenita.
43 Doswell, Thos. W., b. f. **Young Grace**, Eolus, Grace Darling.
44 Doswell, Thos. W., b. f., **Marianne**, Great Tom, Buttress.
45 Dwyer Bros., b. c., **Blacklock**, Billet, Jaconet.
46 Dwyer Bros., b. c. **Hempstead**, Hindoo, Emma Hanly.
47 Dwyer Bros., b. c. **Hannibal**, Hindoo, Mercedes.
48 Dwyer Bros., b. c. **Baychester**, Luke Blackburn, Silvermaid.
49 Dwyer Bros., b. c. **Great Guns**, Great Tom, Mariposa.
50 Dwyer Bros., br. c. **Bush Bolt**, Himyar, Booty.
51 Dwyer Bros., b. c. **Himlex**, Himyar, War Reel.
52 Dwyer Bros., blk. f. ———, Hindoo, Katie.
53 Empire Stable, ch. f. **Landscape**, Woodlands, Artifice.
54 Empire Stable, ch. f. **Clover**, Milner, Fedalma.
55 Eureka Stable, b. f. **Bitter Sweet**, Bersan, Sweetheart.
56 Gray & Co., ch. f. **Barthena**, Faustus, Bothnia.
57 Gray & Co., b. c., **Menthol**, Faustus, Lida Laroy.
58 Greener, Jno. G., ch. f. **Eugenie**, Enquirer, Miss Harding.
59 Hanover Stable, ch. c. ———, Spendthrift, Sinaloa.
60 Hanson, W. B., br. c. **W. B. H.**, Enquirer, Babee.
61 Hearst, Geo., blk. f. **Firework**, Falsetto, Explosion.
62 Hearst, Geo., ch. c. **Algernon**, Joe Daniels, Faustina.
63 Hearst, Geo., ch. f. **Babicora**, Hyder Ali, Graciosa.
64 Hearst, Geo., b. c. **War Path**, Ban Fox or Warwick, Second Hand.
65 Hearst, Geo., ch. c. **Atlas**, Hyder Ali, Fidelity.
66 Hearst, Geo., ch. c. **Anarchist**, Joe Hooker, Chestnut Bell.
67 Hearst, Geo., ch. c. **Snow Ball**, Joe Hooker, Laura Winston.
68 Hearst, Geo., ch. c. **Primero**, Powhatten, Speed.
69 Hearst, Geo., b. c. **Yosemite**, Hyder Ali, Nellie Collier.
70 Hough Bros., ch. f. ———, Enquirer, Melita.
71 Hough Bros., b. f. **Queer Girl**, Himyar, Queen Ban.
72 Israel, E. L., ch. f. **Harpy**, Onondaga, Flora.
73 Israel, E. L., ch. f. ———, Iroquois, Valerian.
74 Kernaghan, G. H. br. f. **Dodo**, Falsetto, Brocade.
75 Leach, Geo. T., blk. c. ———, Vocalic, Francis L.
76 Littlefield, Chas., b. f. **Miss Himyar**, Himyar, Dixietta.
77 McClelland, Byron, ch. f. **Sallie McClelland**, Hindoo, Red and Blue.
78 McCoy, Chas. D., ch. g. **Capt. Wagener**, Great Tom, Sudie McNairy.
79 McElmeel, E., ch. c. ———, Bend'Or, Eusebia.
80 McMahon & Co., ch. f. **Emma J.**, Stratford, Roulette.
81 Madison Stable, ch. g. **Austral**, Reform, Australind.
82 Madison Stable, b. f. **Penitent**, Pardee, Essayez II.
83 Madison Stable, br. f. **Bonita**, Dalnacardoch, Preciosa.
84 Maltese Villa S. F., br. f. **Romeetta**, Woodlands, Dizzy Blonde.
85 Morris, G. B., b. g. **Cerebus**, Luke Blackburn, Glen Hop.
86 Morris, J. A. & A. H., b. c. **Woodcutter**, Forester, Glendalia.
87 Morris, J. A. & A. H., b. c. **Blithe**, Onondaga, Bliss.
88 Morris, J. A. & A. H., ch. c. **Dr. Hasbrouck**, Sir Modred, Sweetbriar.
89 Morris, J. A. & A. H., b. c. **Russell**, Eolus, Tillie Russell.
90 Morris, J. A. & A. H., br. f. **Ambulance**, Onondaga, Black Maria.
91 Morris, J. A. & A. H.; b. f. **Vacation**, Tom Ochiltree, Minnie Mc.
92 Morris, J. A. & A. H., ch. f. **Reckon**, Pizarro, Perhaps.
93 Morris, J. A. & A. H., b. f. **Persistence**, Sir Modred, Parthenia.
94 Morris, J. A. & A. H., b. f. **Correction**, Himyar, Mannie Grey.
95 Morris, J. A. & A. H., b. f. **Truth**, Rotherhill or Bersan, Virtue.

96 Mulholland, J. N., b. f. **Fonda**, Faustus, Ella Payne.
97 Palo Alto, S. F., ch. c. **Rinfax**, Argyle, Amelia.
98 Palo Alto, S. F., ch. f. **Tearless**, Wildidle, Teardrop.
99 Preakness Stable, b. f. **Lizzette**, Hindoo, Bonnie Lizzie.
100 Pulsifer, D. T., ch. c. **Sir George**, Spendthrift, Piccadilly.
101 Pulsifer, D. T., ch. c. **Judge Mitchell**, Stratford, Heatherbelle.
102 Pulsifer, D. T., b. c. **Kirkover**, Atilla, The Squaw.
103 Ramapo Stable, b. c. **John Lackland**, Runnymede, Soubrette.
104 Rancocas Stable, b. c. **Uncertainty**, Emperor, Quandary.
105 Rancocas Stable, b. c. **Sirocco**, Emperor, Breeze.
106 Rancocas Stable, b. f. **Vanity**, Rotherhill or Glenelg, Pride.
107 Rancocas Stable, b. f. **Heiress**, Rotherhill, Finance.
108 Rancocas Stable, b. f. **Arrogance**, Emperor, Disdain.
109 Rancocas Stable, br. c. **Cyrus**, Emperor, Cyrilla.
110 Reed, Chas. & Sons, b. c. **Sextus**, Long Taw, Belle of the Meade.
111 Reed, Chas. & Sons, b. c. **Fairview**, Forester, Wissabickon.
112 Riley, B., br. f. **Seabird**, Sensation, Fiona.
113 Rose, L. J., br. c., **Oscar**, Wildidle, Petroleuse.
114 Sands, W. H., b. c. ——, Kyrle Daly, Trellis.
115 Santa Anita Stable, ch. c. **El Carman**, Gano. Grey Annie.
116 Santa Anita Stable, b. c. **San Joaquin**, Longfellow, Santa Anita Belle.
117 Santa Anita Stable, b. f. **Esperanza**, Grinstead, Hermosa.
118 Santa Anita Stable, ch. c. **Silverado**, Rutherford, Josie C.
119 Santa Anita Stable, b. f. **Lucienga**, Grinstead, Jennie D.
120 Santa Anita Stable, b. f. **Cleopatra**, Grinstead, Maggie Emerson.
121 Scott, W. L., b. c. **Versatile**, Rayon d'Or, Valleria.
122 Scott, W. L., ch. c. **Bolero**, Rayon d'Or, All Hands Around.
123 Scott, W. L., b. c. **Vagabond**, Wanderer, Vivid.
124 Scott, W. L., b. c. **Pestilence**, Wanderer, Quarantine.
125 Scott, W. L., ch. c. **Rushlight**, Wanderer. Blue Cap.
126 Scott, W. L., ch. f. **Seashore**, Wanderer, Li-on.
127 Scott, W. L., b. f. **Wendaway**, Wanderer, Waitaway.
128 Scott, W. L., ch. f. **Millrace**, Wanderer, Santa Lucia.
129 Scott, W. L., b. f. **Tudie**, Wanderer, Clemency.
130 Street, S. W., ch. c. **Borough**, Kantaka, Ione.
131 Sunol Stable, b. g. **Serapis**, Duke of Montrose, Perfecto.
132 Walbaum, G., gr. c. **Gray Rock**, Blazes, Emma II.
133 Walden, Jeter, b. c. **Ely**, Elias Lawrence, Lady Kelley.
134 Walden, Jeter, blk. f. **Favora**, Himyar, Favoress.
135 Walker, Wm., b. c. **Silver Prince**, Spendthrift, Phoebe Mayflower.
136 Walker, Wm., b. c. **Sydney**, Spendthrift, Constantinople.
137 Warnke, H. & Son, ch. c. **Forward**, Farandole, Tambourine.
138 Warnke, H. & Son, ch. c. **King Iro**, Iroquois, Tallulah.

To be run under the auspices of the American Jockey Club.

THIRD RACE.—WITHERS STAKES, for three years old. A sweepstakes of $100 each, h.f., or $20 if declared by July 1st, 1889, with $2,000 added, of which $300 to second, and $100 to third. Winners in 1890 of $2,000 to carry 3 lbs.; of two such races, or one of $3,500, 7 lbs.; of two races of $3,500, 10 lbs. extra. Non-winners of a sweepstakes for three years old allowed 5 lbs.; maidens allowed 10 lbs. Closed August 15th, 1888, with 139 entries. **One Mile.**

Old Scale of Weight.

1 Appleby & Johnson, ch. c. ——, Falsetto, Queen Victoria.
2 Appleby & Johnson, b. c. ——, King Alfonso, Traviata.*
3 Auburndale Stable, ch. c. **King Hazem**, King Ban, Hazem.
4 Bathgate, Chas. W., ch. g. ——, Luke Blackburn, Longitude.
5 Belmont, August, b. c. **Clarendon**, St. Blaise, Clara.
6 Belmont, August, ch. c. **Padishah**, St. Blaise, Sultana.

7 Belmont, August, ch. c. **Chesapeake**, St. Blaise, Susquehanna.
8 Belmont, August, ch. c. **St. Carlo**, St. Blaise, Carina.
9 Belmont, August, ch. c. **St. James**, St. Blaise, Nellie James.†
10 Belmont, August, ch. c. **Belisarius**, St. Blaise, Bella.
11 Belmont, August, b. c. **Lord Dalmeny**, The Ill Used, Lady Rosebery.
12 Belmont, August, b. c. **Magnate**, The Ill Used, Magnetism.
13 Belmont, August, ch. c. **Forest Glen**, The Ill Used, Woodbine.*
14 Belmont, August, ch. c. **Bellerophon**, Kingfisher, Bellona.
15 Bowie, Oden, b. c. **Lordlike**, Vassal, Ladylike.
16 Bowie, Oden, ch. c. **Tennessean**, Vassal, Tennessee.
17 Brown, Ed. (Melbourne Stable), b. c. **Prodigal Son**, Pat Malloy, Homeward Bound.
18 Brown, S. S., b. c. ——, Geo. Kinney, Matinee.
19 Bryant, Sam'l (Melbourne Stable), b. c. **Flambeau**, Forester, Bounce.
20 Byrnes, M. (Melbourne Stable), br. c. **Fernwood**, Falsetto, Quickstep.
21 Byrnes, M. (Melbourne Stable), b. c. **Hawkstone**, Hindoo, Queen Maud.
22 Campbell, Rob't, b. c. **King Charlie**, Prince Charlie, Manola.
23 Castle Stable, b. g. **Felix**, Kingfisher, Felicia.*
24 Castle Stable, ch. c. **Elkton**, Eolus, Helen.
25 Castle Stable, ch. g. ——, Milner, Maggie C.*
26 Castle Stable, b. c. ——, King Ernest, Cadence.*
27 Castle Stable, b. c. **Elmstone**, Stonehenge, Majority.
28 Conner, Wm. M., blk. c. **Dalsyrian**, Dalnacardoch, Syria.
29 Conner, Wm. M., b. c. **Kyelwin**, Kyrle Daly, Mariposa.*
30 Cotton & Boyle, b. c. ——, Joe Hooker, Kitten.
31 Cotton & Boyle, ch. c. ——, Kyrle Daly, Bessie Peyton.
32 Crawford & Roche, b. f. **Alby**, Glengarry, Dublin Belle.
33 Dahlman, I. H. (W. L. Scott), ch. c. **Nashota**, Rayon d'Or, Liatunah.
34 Davis & Hall, ch. c. **Bavarian**, Longfield, Bavaria.
35 Davis & Hall, b. c. ——, Fadladeen, Betsy.
36 Dwyer Bros., ch. c. **Tip Top**, Great Tom, Mozelle.*
37 Dwyer Bros., b. c. **Last Chance**, Virgil, Regan.*
38 Dwyer Bros., blk. c. ——, Virgil, Finework.
39 Dwyer Bros., br. c. **Houston**, Hindoo, Bourbon Belle.
40 Dwyer Bros., b. c. **Blue Bird**, Billet, Mundane.
41 Dwyer Bros., br. c. **Courtland**, Hindoo, Katie.*
42 Dwyer Bros., ch. c. **Frisco**, Hindoo, Francesca.*
43 Dwyer Bros., ch. c. ——, Onondaga, Beatrice.*
44 Dwyer Bros., ch. c. **Last King**, King Ban, Puzzle.
45 Dwyer Bros., b. c. **Sir John**, Sir Modred, Marian.
46 Gideon, D. (John D. Morrissey), ch. c. **Vassar**, Tom Ochiltree, Jenny McKinny.*
47 Gratz, W. (Melbourne Stable), b. c. **Middlestone**, Billet, Bettie Lewis.
48 Hearst, Geo., b. c. **Lancelot**, Sir Modred, Faustina.
49 Hearst, Geo., b. c. **Ballarat**, Sir Modred, La Favorita.
50 Hearst, Geo., b. c. **King Thomas**, King Ban, Maud Hampton.
51 Hearst, Geo., b. c. **Lovelace**, Kyrle Daly, My Love.
52 Hearst, Geo., br. c. **Tournament**, Sir Modred, Plaything.
53 Hearst, Geo., br. c. **Kingmaker**, Warwick, Sister to Jim Douglass
54 Hearst, Geo., ch. c. **Mistral**, Hock Hocking, Maid of the Mist.†
55 Hearst, Geo., ch. c. **Baggage**, Kyrle Daly, Maria F
56 Hearst, Geo., b. c. **Anaconda**, Spendthrift, Maid of Athol.
57 Hearst, Geo., b. f. **Golden Horn**, Spendthrift, Constantinople.
58 Hearst, Geo., b. f. **Gloaming**, Sir Modred, Twilight.
59 Hearst, Geo., b. f. **Valetta**, Warwick, Mileta.
60 Hearst, Geo., ch. f. **Barn Dance**, Warwick, Cinderella.
61 Hearst, Geo., blk. f. **Everglade**, Iroquois, Agenoria.
62 Henry, John (Melbourne Stable), b. c. **Binscarth**, Billet, Lucille Western.*
63 Henry, John (Melbourne Stable), ch. c. **Strathclair**, Onondaga, Lady Stockwell.
64 Hough Bros. (B. Riley), blk. c. **Burlington**, Powhattan, Invercauld.
65 Jennings, W. B. (W. P. Burch) (G. B. Morris) b. c. **Glenscot**, Glenelg, Queen of Scots.*
66 Jennings, W. B., ch. c. ——, Onondaga, Ballet.
67 Jennings, Wm., b. c. **Wyndham**, Warwick, Lorilla.

68 Kraemer & Pryor, br. c. **Gramercy**, Emperor, Felicity.
69 Labold Bros. (Melbourne Stable), b. c. **Sunderland**, Onondaga, Imogene.*
70 Labold Bros. (Melbourne Stable), b. or br. c. **Chevron**, Duke of Magenta, Kaskaskia.*
71 Lakeland, Wm. (A. J. Cassatt) (Wm. Walker) (Melbourne Stable), b. c. **Phœnix**, Mr. Pickwick, Bonnie Wood.
72 Lewis & Long, b. or br. c. **Cadaverous**, Miser, Tipperary Girl.
73 Lorillard, L. L., ch. c. **Sleipner**, Mortemer, Breeze.
74 McClelland, Byron, b. c. **Sam Morse**, Leonatus, Scramble.*
75 McDonald, J. E., ch. c. ——, Prince Charlie, La Favorita.
76 McMahon, Wm., ch. c. **Volo**, Rayon d'Or, Voila.
77 McStea, O. B. (Wm. Walker) (Melbourne Stable), ch. c. **Heatherton**, Hindoo, Sungleam.
78 Madison Stable, b. f. **Laurentia**, Fiddlesticks or Kingfisher or St. Blaise, Laurette.†
79 Madison Stable, b. f. **Tocsin**, Alarm, Auricula.*
80 Madison Stable, b. f. **Sonora**, Spendthrift, Sinaloa.*
81 Madison Stable, ch. f. **Ballad**, Greenland, Sonnet.*
82 Madison Stable, b. c. **Devotee**, Alarm, Sister of Mercy.
83 Madison Stable, ch. c. **Prosit**, Springbok, Venora.*
84 Madison Stable, b. c. **Australitz**, Greenland, Australina.†
85 Madison Stable, b. c. **Iago**, Bend'Or, Billet Doux.
86 Madison Stable, br. c. **Australand**, Reform, Australind.†
87 Maltese Villa Stock Farm, b. c. **Abdiel**, Jocko, Cousin Peggy.
88 Maltese Villa Stock Farm, b. c. **Achilles**, Norfolk, Thetis.*
89 Melbourne Stable, ch. c. **Palisade**, Powhattan, Indemnity.
90 Morris, G. B., b. c. **Lisimony**, Lisbon, Patrimony.
91 Morris, G. B., ch. c. **Jersey Pat**, Pat Malloy, Jersey Lass.
92 Morris, J. A. & A. H., ch. c. **Cayuga**, Iroquois. Letola.
93 Morris, J. A. & A. H., br. c. **Mucilage**, Kyrle Daly, Mura.
94 Morris, J. A. & A. H., br. c. **Dr. Helmuth**, Sir Modred, Sweetbriar.
95 Morris, J. A. & A. H., ch. c. **King's Own**, Hopeful, Queen's Own.
96 Morris, J. A. & A. H., b. c. **Telephone**, Glenelg, Acoustic.
97 Morris, J. A. & A. H., br. f. **Starlight**, Iroquois, Vandalite.
98 Morris, J. A. & A. H., ch. f. **Winsome**, Kyrle Daly, Winnifred.*
99 Morris, J. A. & A. H., ch. f. **Constellation**, Tom Ochiltree, Minnie Mc.*
100 Morris, J. A. & A. H., b. f. **Lady McNairy**, Duke of Magenta, Sudie McNairy.*
101 Morris, J. A. & A. H., ch. f. **Homeopathy**, Reform, Maggie B. B.
102 Murphy, Dennis (Madison Stable), b. or br. f. **Vera**, Greenland, Maggie J.†
103 Murphy, Dennis (Madison Stable), ch. c. **Ganador**, Greenland, Patti.†
104 Newton, H. A. (Melbourne Stable), b. or br. c. **Fakofan**, Falsetto, Patula.†
105 Pincus, J., gr. c. **Bluestone**, Falsetto, Geneva.
106 Pincus, J., ch. f. ——, King Ban, Flora.
107 Preakness Stable, b. c. **Dundee**, Macduff, Virginia Bush.
108 Preakness Stable, b. c. **Windsor**, Warwick or Sir Modred, Lady Middleton.
109 Riley, B., b. c. **Barnegat**, Billet, Emma Hanly.
110 Santa Anita Stable, b. c. **Clio**, Grinstead. Glenita.
111 Santa Anita Stable, ch. c. **Honduras**, Grinstead, Jennie B.
112 Santa Anita Stable, br. c. **Costa Rica**, Grinstead, Althola.
113 Santa Anita Stable, b. c. **San Diego**, Grinstead, Clara D.
114 Santa Anita Stable, ch. c. **Amigo**, Prince Charlie, Mission Belle.
115 Santa Anita Stable, b. f. ——, Glenelg, Malta.
116 Scott, W. L., ch. c. **Chaos**, Rayon d'Or, Lilly R.
117 Scott, W. L., ch. c. **Leighton**, Rayon d'Or, L'Argentine.
118 Scott, W. L., ch. c. **Franco**, Rayon d'Or, Florio.
119 Scott, W. L., b. g. **Banquet**, Rayon d'Or, Ella T.
120 Scott, W. L., ch. g. **Maximus**, Reform, Rachel.
121 Scott, W. L., ch. c. **Torso**, Algerine, Santa Lucia.
122 Scott, W. L., b. c. **Index**, Kantaka, Sheboygan.*
123 Scott, W. L., ch. c. **Canteen**, Kantaka, Maurine.
124 Scott, W. L., b. c. **Zor**, Kantaka, Lady Scarborough.
125 Scott, W. L., ch. f. **Paradox**, Rayon d'Or, Lizzie Cox.
126 Stuart, James, ch. c. ——, Stonehenge, Mary Buckley.‡
127 Taylor, Frank (W. L. Scott), ch. c. **Centaur**, Rayon d'Or, Luella.

128 Walker, M. (Melbourne Stable), ch. c. **Coleraine**, Hindoo, Waif.
129 Walker, Wm. (Melbourne Stable), ch. c. **Foxmede**, Falsetto, Britomarte.
130 Walker, Wm. (Chas. Jordan) (Melbourne Stable), ch. c. **Frontenac**, Falsetto, Lerna.
131 Weir, P. T. (W. L. Scott), ch. c. **Rafter**, Kantaka, Belle of Maywood.
132 Williams, J. S. (W. L. Scott), ch. c. **Crawfish**, Rayon d'Or, Brenda.
133 Withers, D. D., b. c. ——, Uncas, Chamois.
134 Withers, D. D., br. c. ——, Uncas, Sweet Home.
135 Withers, D. D., b. c. ——, King Ernest, Cyclone.
136 Withers, D. D., b. c. ——, Stonehenge, Eccola.
137 Withers, D. D., b. c. ——, Stonehenge, Adage.
138 Withers, D. D., b. c., ——, Kinglike, Fanfan.
139 Withers, D. D., ch. c. ——, Kinglike, Maxim.

* Declared July 1, 1889.   † Declared since July 1, 1889.   ‡ Void.

FOURTH RACE. — NEW YORK JOCKEY CLUB HANDICAP, for all ages.

A sweepstakes of $150 each, h.f., or only $25 if declared by 4 P.M. on the day before the day appointed for the race, with $5,000 added, of which $1,000 to second, and $500 to third. Weights to be published on the second day before the race. Closed January 2d, 1890, with 68 entries.

One Mile and a Quarter.

1 Armstrong, S. P., b. h. **Juggler**, 5, Jils Johnson, Avoca.
2 Belmont, August, b. g. **Raceland**, 5, Billet, Calomel.
3 Belmont, August, ch. g., **Chesapeake**, 3, St. Blaise, Susquehanna.
4 Belmont, August, ch. h **Prince Royal**, 5, Kingfisher, Princess.
5 Belmont, August, b. f. **Fides**, 4, The Ill Used, Fillette.
6 Beverwyck Stable, b. m. **Lavinia Belle**, 5, Longfellow, Belle Knight.
7 Beverwyck Stable, br. f. **Brown Princess**. 4, Prince Charlie, Nannie Black.
8 Brown, S. S., br. f. **Senorita**, 4, Prince Charlie, Gondola.
9 Brown, S. S., br. c. **Reporter**, 4, Enquirer, Bonnie Meade.
10 Brown, S. S., br. c. **Buddhist**, 4. Hindoo. Emma Hanly.
11 Brown, S. S., ch. c. **Cortez**, 4, King Alfonso. Invercauld.
12 Carter, John J., ch. c. **Kasson**, 4, Springbok, Edith.
13 Castle Stable, b. c. **Diablo**, 4, Eolus, Grace Darling.
14 Cotton, J., b. c. **Carroll**, 4, Billet, Juanita.
15 Davis & Hall, gr. h. **Oriflamme**, 6, Flood, Frolic.
16 Dwyer Bros., br. h. **Kingston**, 6, Spendthrift, Kapanga.
17 Dwyer Bros., b. c. **Longstreet**, 4, Longfellow, Semper Idem.
18 Dwyer Bros., b. h. **Sir Dixon**, 5, Billet, Jaconet.
19 Dwyer Bros., b. c. **Blackburn**, 3, Luke Blackburn, Tomboy.
20 Dwyer Bros., ch. h. **Hanover**, 6, Hindoo, Bourbon Belle.
21 Empire Stable, br. c. **Madstone**, 4, Vanderbilt, Nina Turner.
22 Empire Stable, ch. c. **Tormentor**, 3, Joe Hooker, Callie Smart.
23 Haggin, J. B., b. m. **Firenzi**, 6, Glenelg, Florida.
24 Haggin, J. B., br. c. **Fitz-James**, 5, Kyrle Daly, Electra.
25 Haggin, J. B., ch. c. **Salvator**, 4, Prince Charlie, Salina.
26 Hart, L., b. f., **Maggie K**, 3, Billet, Miss Annie.
27 Hearst, Geo., ch. c. **Rhono**, 4, Flood, Rosetta.
28 Hearst, Geo., blk. m. **Gorgo**, 5, Isonomy, Flirt.
29 Hearst, Geo., b. c. **King Thomas**, 3, King Ban, Maud Hampton.
30 Hearst, Geo., br. c. **Tournament**, 3, Sir Modred, Plaything.
31 Hearst, Geo., b. c. **Anaconda**, 3, Spendthrift, Maid of Athol.
32 Hearst, Geo., ch. c. **imp Del Mar**, 4, Somnes, Maid of the Hills.
33 Hearst, Geo., b. c. **Almont**, 4, Three Cheers, Question.
34 Hough Bros., b. g. **Come to Taw**, 4, Long Taw, Mollie Seabrook.
35 Labold Bros., br. c. **Experience**, 3, Prince Charlie, Myralia.
36 Labold Bros., br. f. **Retrieve**, 4, Duke of Montrose, Patti.

37 Labold Bros., br. h. **Montrose**, 6, Duke of Montrose, Patti.
38 Lakeland, Wm., b. h. **Exile**, a, Mortemer, Second Hand.
39 Lakeland. Wm., ch. h. **Tea Tray**, 5, Rayon d'Or, Ella T.
40 Littlefield, Chas., b. c. **Jubal**, 4, Jils Johnson, Avoca.
41 Lloyd, L., ch. g. **St. Luke**, a, Botheration, Mabel.
42 McKane, R. ch. c. **Cracksman**, 4, Woodlands, Sue Ryder.
43 Maltese Villa S. F., b. c. **Flood-Tide**, 4, Flood, Lady Evangeline.
44 Montana Stables, ch. c. **Spokane**, 4, Hyder Ali, Interpose.
45 Morris, G. B., ch. h. **Taragon**, 5, Stratford, Tara.
46 Morris, G. B., b. c. **Eric**, 4, Duke of Magenta, Second Hand.
47 Morris, J. A. & A. H., ch. c. **Cayuga**, 3, Iroquois, Letola.
48 Morris, J. A. & A. H., ch. c. **King's Own**, 3, Hopeful, Queen's Own.
49 Mullins, J., b. h. **Badge**, 5, The Ill Used, The Baroness.
50 New York Stable, b. c. **Successor**, 3, Vauxhall, Sequence.
51 Preakness Stable, ch. g. **Montague**, 5, Mortemer, Evadne.
52 Pulsifer, D. T., b. c. **Donley**, 4, Longfellow, Pearl Tyler.
53 Pulsifer, D. T., b. c. **Tenny**, 4, Rayon d'Or, Belle of Maywood.
54 Pulsifer, D. T., ch. h. **Brother Ban**, 6, King Ban, War Reel.
55 Ramapo Stable, ch. h. **Charley Dreux**, 5, Eolus, Lizzie Hazlewood.
56 Reed, Chas. & Sons, blk. c. **Viking**, 4, Fechter, Thora.
57 Santa Anita Stable, ch. m. **Los Angeles**, 5, Glenelg, La Polka.
58 Santa Anita Stable, b. c. **Santiago**, 3, Grinstead, Clara D.
59 Santa Anita Stable, ch. c. **Honduras**, 3, Grinstead, Jennie B.
60 Santa Anita Stable, ch. c. **Amigo**, 3, Prince Charlie, Mission Belle.
61 Santa Anita Stable, b. c. **Clio**, 3, Grinstead, Glenita.
62 Stewart, Jno. T. & Son, ch. f. **Verdeur**, 4, Vandal Jr. or Democrat, Minnie K.
63 Street, S. W., br. c. **Sentiment**, 4, Sensation, Aella.
64 Stuart, Louis & Co., b. h. **Tristan**, 5, Glenelg, Traviata.
65 Western Union Stable, b. c. **Persuader**, 4, Dickens, Persuasion.
66 Western Union Stable, b. h. **Dunboyne**, 6, Uncas, Frey
67 Withers, D. D., br. c. **Major Domo**, 4, Tom Ochiltree, Sweet Home.
68 Withers, D. D., br. c. **Cynosure**, 4, Tom Ochiltree, Cyclone.

FIFTH RACE. — For two years old. A sweepstakes of $15 each, with $750 added, of which $100 to second, and $50 to third. The winner to be sold at auction for $2,000; if entered to be sold for less, 1 lb. allowed for each $100 down to $1,000; then 2 lbs. for each $100 down to $500. **Five Furlongs.**

SIXTH RACE. — For three years old and upward. A sweepstakes of $15 each, with $750 added, of which $100 to second, and $50 to third. The winner to be sold at auction for $3,000; if entered to be sold for less, 1 lb. allowed for each $100 down to $500. **One Mile.**

Centre of Grand Stand

SECOND DAY.—SATURDAY, MAY 31ST.

FIRST RACE. — For three years old and upward. A sweepstakes of $15 each, with $750 added, of which $100 to second, and $50 to third. Winners in 1889 or 1890 of $3,000 to carry 5 lbs. extra; twice of $3,000, or once of $5,000, 7 lbs. extra. Nonwinners in 1889 or 1890 of $2,000 allowed 5 lbs.; of $1,000, 7 lbs. Maidens, if three years old, allowed 12 lbs.; if four and upward, 20 lbs. **One Mile and a Furlong.**

SECOND RACE.—FERNCLIFF WELTER HANDICAP, for three years old and upward. A sweepstakes of $20 each, or $5 if declared, with $1,000 added, of which $200 to second, and $100 to third. Entries to be made on Thursday, May 29th. Weights to be announced and declarations to be made on Friday, May 30th. **Five Furlongs.**

THIRD RACE. — DEBUTANTE STAKES, for fillies two years old. A sweepstakes of $50 each, h.f., or only $10 if declared by April 1st, with $1,250 added, of which $250 to second, and $100 to third. Winners excluded from starting and not to pay forfeit. Closed January 2d, 1890, with 117 entries. **Five Furlongs.**

1 Auburndale Stable, ch. f. ———, Onondaga, Gleam.
2 Barbee, Geo., ch. f. **Coquette,** Fonso, Ardente.
3 Belmont, August, ch. f. **La Tosca,** St. Blaise, Toucques.
4 Belmont, August, ch. f. **Beauty,** St. Blaise, Bella.
5 Belmont, August, ch. f. **Flavia,** St. Blaise, Flavina.
6 Belmont, August, ch. f. **Belligerent,** Fiddlesticks, Bellona.
7 Beverwyck Stable, b. f. **Polly S.,** Pizarro, Amadine.
8 Beverwyck Stable, b. f. **Bertha Campbell,** King Alfonso, Vulpine.
9 Beverwyck Stable, b. f. **Come and Go,** Alarm, Heel and Toe.
10 Beverwyck Stable, ch. f. **Hansa,** Fellowcraft, Hanap.
11 Beverwyck Stable, b. f. **Lottie,** Faustus, Loretto.
12 Brown, S. S., ch. f. ———, Himyar, Jewel.
13 Brown, S. S., ch. f. ———, Richmond, Ellen Alice.
14 Bruce, L. C., br. f. **Vocaletta,** Vocalic, Vietta.
15 Bruce, L. C., b. f. **Krikina,** Muscovy, Krik.
16 Castle Stable, b. f. **Pert,** Glenelg, Silk Gown.
17 Clover Stable, br. f. **Margherita,** Rossifer, Certiorari.
18 Clover Stable, ch. f. **Sarah Hall,** Stratford, Minnie Andrews.
19 Conner, Wm. M., ch. f. **Furlano,** Woodlands, Waltz.
20 Conner, Wm. M., ch. f. **Gardelia,** Woodlands, Glidelia.
21 Conner, Wm. M., b. f. **Imperieuse,** Pizarro, Imogene.
22 Conner, Wm. M., br. f. **Beata,** Strathmore, Beatrice.
23 Corrigan, Ed., br. f. **Corine Buckingham,** Powhattan, Hattie Harris.
24 Daly, John, ch. f. - —-, Joe Daniels, Mottle.
25 Daly, Marcus, ch. f. **Bonnie Lass,** Sir Modred, Bonnie Kate.
26 Daly, Marcus, ch. f. **Leonora,** Sir Modred, Lizzie Lucas.
27 Daly, Marcus, b. f. **Mistletoe,** Sir Modred, Letola.
28 Daly, Marcus, b. f. **Namouna,** Sir Modred, La Favorita.
29 Daly, W. C., b. f. **Lizzie,** St. Blaise, Fenfollet.

30 Davis & Hall, ch. f. **Euna**, Gaberlunzie, Eunice.
31 Davis & Hall, b. f. **Gaiety**, Gaberlunzie, Kenita.
32 Doswell, Thos. W., b. f. **Young Grace**, Eolus, Grace Darling.
33 Dwyer Bros., blk. f. ——, Hindoo, Katie.
34 Dwyer Bros., b. f. ——, Hindoo, Bourbon Belle.
35 Dwyer Bros., ch. f. **Ada C.**, Himyar, Adonia.
36 Empire Stable, ch. f. **Landscape**, Woodlands, Artifice.
37 Empire Stable, ch. f. **Clover**, Milner, Fedalma.
38 Enreka Stable, b. f. **Bitter Sweet**, Bersan, Sweetheart.
39 Graham, J. R., b. f. **Florence**, Warwick, Ysabel.
40 Gray & Co., b. f. **Lenore**, Faustus, Peggy Woods.
41 Gray & Co., b. f. **Betty Prather**, Faustus, Zula.
42 Gray & Co., ch. f. **Barthena**, Faustus, Bothnia.
43 Greener, Jno. G., ch. f. **Eugenie**, Enquirer, Miss Harding.
44 Hanover Stable, ch. f. ——, Neptune, Alma.
45 Hanover Stable, b. f. ——, Luke Blackburn, Vintage Time.
46 Hearst, Geo., blk. f. **Firework**, Falsetto, Explosion.
47 Hearst, Geo., ch. f. **Babicora**, Hyder Ali, Graciosa.
48 Hough Bros., ch. f. ——, Enquirer, Melita.
49 Hough Bros., b. f. **Queer Girl**, Himyar, Queen Ban.
50 Hunter, John, blk. f. **Ortawin**, Onondaga, Annette.
51 Hunter, John, b. f. **Mayflower**, Iroquois, Blue Gown.
52 Israel, E. L., ch. f. **Harpy**, Onondaga, Flora.
53 Israel, E. L., ch. f. ——, Iroquois, Valerian.
54 Jennings, W. B., ch. f. ——, Onondaga, Matagorda.
55 Jennings, Wm., br. f. **Mary Stone**, Sir Modred, Rosemary.
56 Kernaghan, G. H., br. f. **Dodo**, Falsetto, Brocade.
57 Kernaghan, G. H., b. f. ——, Duke of Montrose, Helen Wallace.
58 Kernaghan, G. H., b. f. ——, Lisbon, Bertha B.
59 Kneale, James, b. f. **Miss Williams**, Himyar, Grace Lee.
60 Lakeland, Wm., b. f. **Modjeska**, Glenelg, Madame Dudley.
61 Littlefield, C., b. f. **Miss Himyar**, Himyar, Dixietta.
62 McClelland, Byron, ch. f. **Sallie McClelland**, Hindoo, Red and Blue.
63 McClelland, Byron, br. f. ——, Billet, Retreat.
64 McCoy, C. D., br. f. **Kittie T.**, Enquirer, Bonnie Lawn.
65 McElmeel, E., b. f. ——, Stratford, Manmee.
66 Madison Stable, b. f. **Penitent**, Pardee, Essayez II.
67 Madison Stable, br. f. **Bonita**, Dalnacardoch, Preciosa.
68 Maltese Villa S. F., br. f. **Romeetta**, Woodlands, Dizzy Blonde.
69 Morris, J. A. & A. H., br. f. **Ambulance**, Onondaga, Black Maria.
70 Morris, J. A. & A. H., b. f. **Persistence**, Sir Modred, Parthenia.
71 Morris, J. A. & A. H., ch. f. **Reckon**, Pizarro, Perhaps.
72 Morris, J. A. & A. H., b. f. **Vacation**, Tom Ochiltree, Minnie Mc.
73 Morris, J. A. & A. H., b. f. **Correction**, Himyar, Mannie Grey.
74 Morris, J. A. & A. H., b. f. **Truth**, Rotherhill or Bersan, Virtue.
75 Morris, J. A. & A. H., ch. f. imp **Prosperity**, Zealot, Wealth.
76 Morris, J. A. & A. H., ch. f. **Affection**, St. Blaise, Affinity.
77 Morris, J. A. & A. H., b. f. **Compassion**, Alarm, Sister of Mercy.
78 Mulholland, J. N., ch. f. **Fulda**, Faustus, Can Dance.
79 Palo Alto S. F., ch. f. **Tearless**, Wildidle, Teardrop.
80 Palo Alto S. F., ch. f. **Rosebud**, Wildidle, Rosetta.
81 Preakness Stable, b. f. **Lizzette**, Hindoo, Bonnie Lizzie.
82 Preakness Stable, ch. f. **Flavilla**, Macduff, Vintage.
83 Ramapo Stable, br. f. ——, Iroquois, Guildean.
84 Rancocas Stable, b. f. **Vanity**, Rotherhill or Glenelg, Pride.
85 Rancocas Stable, ch. f. **Lima**, Pizarro, Gladiola.
86 Rancocas Stable, b. f. **Arrogance**, Emperor, Disdain.
87 Reed, Chas. & Sons, b. f. **Annie**, Mr. Pickwick, Bonnie Wood.
88 Reed, Chas. & Sons, ch. f. **Reilly**, Mr. Pickwick, Glencairne.
89 Riley, B., br. f. **Seabird**, Sensation, Fiona.
90 Rollins, W. C., b. f. ——, Gunnar, Annie S.
91 Rose, L. J., b. f. **Flight**, Flood, Flirt.
92 Santa Anita Stable, b. f. **Esperanza**, Grinstead, Hermosa.
93 Santa Anita Stable, b. f. **Cleopatra**, Grinstead, Maggie Emerson
94 Santa Anita Stable, b. f. **Ogarita**, Longfellow, Mission Belle.

95 Santa Anita Stable, b. f. **Lacienga**, Grinstead, Jennie D.
96 Sattler, Chas., b. f. ——, Stratford, Water Lily.
97 Scott, W. L., br. f. **Amulet**, Rayon d'Or, Presto.
98 Scott, W. L., b. f. **Exclusion**, Rayon d'Or, Monopoly.
99 Scott, W. L., ch. f. **Miss Ransom**, Rayon d'Or, Nellie Ransom.
100 Scott, W. L., b. f. **Maywood**, Rayon d'Or, Belle of Maywood.
101 Scott, W. L., ch. f. **Turmoil**, Rayon d'Or, Lilly R.
102 Scott, W. L., ch. f. **Cutalong**, Rayon d'Or, Claudia.
103 Scott, W. L., ch. f. **Millrace**, Wanderer, Santa Lucia.
104 Scott, W. L., b. f. **Fugitive**, Wanderer, Honey Bee.
105 Scott, W. L., b. f. **Tudie**, Wanderer, Clemency.
106 Scott, W. L., b. f. **Wendaway**, Wanderer, Waitaway.
107 Scott, W. L., ch. f. **Seashore**, Wanderer, Lison.
108 Shippee, L. M., b. f. **May II.**. Falsetto, Glenluine.
109 Shippee, L. M., b. f. **False Queen**, Falsetto, Queen Victoria.
110 Smith, J. L., b. f. **Belle Smith**, Keene Jim, Fannie W.
111 Street, S. W., br. f. **Aunt Emma**, Spendthrift, Maid of Athol.
112 Stuart, Louis & Co., b. f. ——, Mr. Pickwick, Acquittal.
113 Union Stable, ch. f. **Polydora**, St. Blaise, Polenta.
114 Walden, Jeter, br. f. **Katrina**, Kyrle Daly or Sir Modred, Miss Laura.
115 Walden, Jeter, blk. f. **Favora**, Himyar, Favoress.
116 Warnke, H. & Son, ch. f. **Clara Lee**, Great Tom, Clara L.
117 Warnke, H. & Son, b. f. **Ella T.**, Himyar, Ella G.

FOURTH RACE. — TOBOGGAN SLIDE HANDICAP,

for all ages. A sweepstakes of $100 each, h.f., or only $20 if declared, the club to guarantee the gross value of the stake to be $10,000, of which $2,000 to second, and $1,000 to third. Weights to be announced February 1st, and declarations to be made by February 20th. Winners after April 1st of two races of any value, or one of $1,500, to carry 4 lbs. extra; of one of $3,000 or two of $2,000, 7 lbs. extra; or two of $3,000 or one of $6,000, 10 lbs. extra. Closed January 2d, 1890, with 119 entries.

Six Furlongs.

1 Dwyer Bros., br. h. **Kingston**, 6, Spendthrift, Kapango * **136**
2 Haggin, J. B., ch. c. **Salvator**, 4, Prince Charlie, Salina * **132**
3 Dwyer Bros., ch. h. **Hanover**, 6, Hindoo, Bourbon Belle * **132**
4 Pulsifer, D. T., b. c. **Tenny**, 4, Rayon d'Or, Belle of Maywood **130**
5 Belmont, August, ch. h. **Prince Royal**, 5, Kingfisher, Princess * . . . **130**
6 Haggin, J. B., b. m. **Firenzi**, 6, Glenelg, Florida * **128**
7 Morris, J. A. & A. H., blk. h. **Britannic**, 6, Plevna, Faithless **127**
8 Scoggan Bros., ch. g. **Proctor Knott**, 4, Luke Blackburn, Tallapoosa . **124**
9 Mullins, J. L., b. h. **Badge**, 5, The Ill Used, The Baroness **124**
10 Gebhard, F., b. g. **Volunteer II.**, 6, Mortemer, Sly Boots **124**
11 Walbaum, G., b. h. **Bradford**, 6, Glengarry or Bramble, Nevada . . . **122**
12 Islip Stable, ch. h. **Strideaway**, 6, Glenmore, Spinaway **122**
13 Hearst, Geo., blk. m. **Gorgo**, 5, Isonomy, Flirt **122**
14 Brown, S. S., br. c. **Reporter**, 4, Enquirer, Bonnie Meade **122**
15 DeLong, J., br. h. **Sam Harper, Jr.**, a, Sam Harper, Lucy Cherry . . **122**
16 Maltese Villa, S. F., ch. m. **Geraldine**, 5, Grinstead, Cousin Peggy . . **122**
17 Santa Anita Stable, ch. m. **Los Angeles**, 5, Glenelg, LaPolka **120**
18 McKane, R., ch. c. **Cracksman**, 4, Woodlands, Sue Ryder **120**
19 Brown, S. S., br. c. **Buddhist**, 4, Hindoo, Emma Hanly **120**
20 Hough Bros., b. g. **Come to Taw**, 4, Long Taw, Mollie Seabrook * . . **118**
21 Sattler, Charles, ch. c. **Gregory**, 3, Macaroon, Abundance **118**
22 McConn, D., br. c. **Loantaka**, 4, Sensation, Peggy Dawdle **118**
23 Dwyer Bros., b. c. **Blackburn**, 3, Luke Blackburn, Tomboy * . . **118**
24 Scott, W. L., ch. g. **Chaos**, 3, Rayon d'Or, Lilly R.* **118**

25 Empire Stable, br. c. **Madstone**, 4, Vanderbilt, Nina Turner **118**
26 Scott, W. L., ch. c. **Torso**, 3, Algerine, Santa Lucia * **118**
27 Gideon, D., b. c., **French Park**, 4, King Ban, Lou Pike **118**
28 Morris, G. B., ch. c. **Tipstaff**, 4, Rayon d'Or or Kantaka, Verdict* . . **116**
29 Brown, S. S., ch. c. **Cortez**, 4, King Alfonso, Invercauld **116**
30 Warnke, H. & Son, blk. f. **Reclare**, 3, Reform, Clara **116**
31 Belmont, August, b. f. **Fides**, 4, The Ill Used, Fillette **116**
32 Belmont, August, b. c. **Magnate**, 3, The Ill Used, Magnetism * **116**
33 Belmont, August, b. c. **Blue Rock**, 4, Billet, Calomel **116**
34 Honig, D. A., br. g. **Cartoon**, 4, Reform, Clara **116**
35 Davis & Hall, b. g. **Patrocles**, a, Kingfisher, Patience * **115**
36 Brown, S. S., ch. h. **Defaulter**, 5, Spendthrift, Authoress **114**
37 Bowie, Oden, ch. m. **Belle d'Or**, 5, Rayon d'Or, Belle Meade **114**
38 Beverwyck Stable, b. c. **Cassius**, 4, Longfellow, Southern Belle **112**
39 New York Stable, b. c. **Successor**, 3, Vauxhall, Sequence **112**
40 Rose, L. J., b. g. **Rico**, 3, Shannon, Lucy **112**
41 Carrigan, Ed., b. g. **G. W. Cook**, 5, Longfellow, Miss Tilton **112**
42 Campbell, R. E., br. c. **Protection**, 3, Prince Charlie, Manola **112**
43 Beverwyck Stable, b. c. **Castaway II.**, 4, Outcast, Lucy Lisle **112**
44 Beverwyck Stable, br. f. **Brown Princess**, 4, Prince Charlie, Nannie
Black **112**
45 Hearst, Geo., b. c. **Ballarat**, 3, Sir Modred, La Favorita **112**
46 Dwyer Bros., br. f. **Aurania**, 4, Virgil, Ann Fief **112**
47 Littlefield, C., ch. g. **My Fellow**, 4, Fellowcraft, Dixietta **112**
48 Gideon, D., b. g. **Stonington**, 4, Hurrah or Pizarro, Quandary **112**
49 Davis & Hall, b. m. **Bess**, a, Fadladeen, Betsy **111**
50 Scott, W. L., ch. c. **Leighton**, 3, Rayon d'Or, L'Argentine * **111**
51 Lloyd, L., ch. g. **St. John**, a, Botheration, dam by Victory **110**
52 Hodges & Austin, b. g. **Sunday**, 6, Ironclad, Nellie Shannon **110**
53 Forbes, Geo., b. h. **Volta**, 5, Virgil, Mollie Hyland **110**
54 Forbes, Geo., b. c. **Cynosure**, 4, Tom Ochiltree, Cyclone **110**
55 Amacker, Wm., ch. f. **Sallie Hagan**, 4, Faustus, Lady Woodford . . **110**
56 Haggin, J. B., br. c. **Fitz James**, 4, Kyrle Daly, Electra **110**
57 Santa Anita Stable, ch. c. **Honduras**, 3, Grinstead, Jennie B. . . . **109**
58 Hearst, Geo., b. c. **Almont**, 4, Three Cheers, Question **109**
59 Hough Bros., b. g. **Forest King**, 4, The Ill Used, Woodbine **109**
60 Empire Stable, ch. c. **Tormentor**, 3, Joe Hooker, Callie Smart . . . **108**
61 Morris, J. A. & A. H., ch. f. **Holiday**, 4, Hopeful, Minnie Mc. . . . **108**
62 Hough Bros., br. c. **Vengeur**, 4, Vandal Jr., Rebecca Rowett **108**
63 Dwyer Bros., b. c. **Sir John**, 3, Sir Modred, Marian **108**
64 Morris, J. A. & A. H., ch. f. **Druidess**, 3, Stonehenge, Castagnette . . **108**
65 Smith, A., b. f., **Lady Reel**, 4, Fellowcraft, Mannie Grey **108**
66 Morris, J. A. & A. H., br. f. **Starlight**, 3, Iroquois, Vandalite **108**
67 Carter, J. J., ch. c. **Kasson**, 4, Springbok, Edith **107**
68 Blunt, Edmund, b. c. **Seymour**, 4, Stratford, Imelda **107**
69 Hough Bros., br. f. **Retrieve**, 4, Duke of Montrose, Patti **107**
70 Bonchurch Stable, b. g. **Serenader**, 5, Leonatus, Serenade **107**
71 Hart, L., b. f. **Maggie K.**, 3, Billet, Miss Annie **107**
72 Hearst, Geo., b. c. **King Thomas**, 3, King Ban, Maud Hampton . . **107**
73 Belmont, August, ch. g. **Chesapeake**, 3, St. Blaise, Susquehanna . . . **107**
74 Davis & Hall, ch. g. **Bavarian**, 3, Longfield, Bavaria * **106**
75 Morris, J. A. & A. H., ch. f. **Homœopathy**, 3, Reform, Maggie B. B. . . **106**
76 Corrigan, Ed., ch. c. **Boodler**, 4, Enquirer, Bribery **106**
77 Castle Stable, blk. f. **Rainbow**, 3, Iroquois, Explosion **106**
78 Pulsifer, D. T., ch. g. **Punster Jr.**, 3, Punster, Maud P. **106**
79 Porter, F. P., ch. m. **Kate Bensberg**, 5, Respond, Mary H. **106**
80 McCoy, C. D., ch. c. **Beck**, 4, Bertram, Addie Hart **106**
81 Scott, W. L., ch. f. **Paradox**, 3, Rayon d'Or, Lizzie Cox **106**
82 Davis & Hall, b. f. **Little Ella**, 3, Little Phil, Ella Warfield **106**
83 Greener, Jno. G., ch. c. **Culprit**, 4, Outcast, Sallie A. **106**
84 Empire Stable, b. g. **Trestle**, 3, Kyrle Daly, Trellis **106**
85 Withers, D. D., b. f. **Stately**, 4, King Ernest, Mimi **106**
86 Western Union Stable, b. c. **Persuader**, 4, Dickens, Persuasion . . . **106**
87 Scoggan Bros., ch. f. **English Lady**, 3, Miser, Bonny Lass **106**
88 Morris, G. B., ch. c. **Jersey Pat**, 3, Pat Malloy, Jersey Lass **106**

Grand Stand Promenade

89 Haggin, J. B., blk. c. **Fresno**, 4, Falsetto, Cachuca	**106**
90 Santa Anita Stable, ch. f. **Sinaloa II**, 3, Grinstead, Maggie Emerson .	**105**
91 Dingley & Spratt, b. g. **Red Elm**, a, Glen Elm, Unknown	**105**
92 Auburndale Stable, ch. c. **King Hazem**, 3, King Ban, Hazem . . .	**105**
93 Belmont, August, b. f. **Amazon**, 3, The Ill Used, Fair Barbarian . . .	**105**
94 Morris, J. A. & A. H., br. c. **Dr. Helmuth**, 3, Sir Modred, Sweetbriar .	**100**
95 Gray & Co., b. c. **Roseberry**, 3, Faustus, Bonnie Rose	**100**
96 Amacker, Wm., ch. c. **Worth**, 3, Luke Blackburn, Peytona Barry . .	**100**
97 Clifton Stable, br. c. **Winfield**, 4, Kyrle Daly, Winifred	**100**
98 Pulsifer, D. T., ch. f. **Coots**, 4, Prince Charlie, Blunder *	**100**
99 Yale Stable, ch. f. **Phoebe**, 3, St. Blaise, Mehallah *	**100**
100 Hearst, Geo., ch. f. **Cosette**, 3, Joe Hooker, Abbie W	**100**
101 Scoggan Bros., ch. c. **Ban Chief**, 3, King Ban, Wigwam *	**100**
102 Ross, J. R., b. f. **Kitty Van**, 4, Vanderbilt, April Fool	**100**
103 Santa Anita Stable, b. c. **Clio**, 3, Grinstead, Glenita	**100**
104 Scoggan Bros., ch. c. **Good-bye**, 3, Hyder Ali, Jenny Rowett * . . .	**100**
105 Scott, W. L., ch. c. **Franco**, 3, Rayon d'Or, Florio *	**100**
106 Santa Anita Stable, ch. c. **Amigo**, 3, Prince Charlie, Mission Bell . .	**100**
107 Hearst, Geo., ch. c., **Imp Del Mar**, 4, Somnes, Maid of the Hills . .	**100**
108 Pincus, J., gr. g. **Granite**, 3, Falsetto, Geneva	**100**
109 Auburndale Stable, ch. m. **Ofalece**, 6, Harry O'Fallon, Sue Finnie . .	**100**
110 Labold Bros., ch. c. **Isaac Lewis**, 3, Prince Charlie, Bellona	**100**
111 Hearst, Geo., b. f. **Gloaming**, 3, Sir Modred, Twilight	**100**
112 Scott, W. L., ch. f. **Martha**, 3, Rayon d'Or, Lucy Wallace *	**100**
113 Hearst, Geo., b. c. **Sir Lancelot**, 3, Sir Modred, Faustina	**100**
114 Sunol Stable, b. c. **Varius**, 3, Virgil, Chinook	**100**
115 Eureka Stable, b. f., **Laurentia**, 3, Kingfisher or Fiddlesticks, or St.	
Blaise, Laurette	**100**
116 Daly, Marcus, b. c. **Prince Charming**, 2, Sir Modred, Carissima . .	**90**
117 Scott, W. L., ch. f. **Seashore**, 2, Wanderer, Lison *	**87**
118 Daly, Marcus, ch. f. **Leonora**, 2, Sir Modred, Lizzie Lucas	**87**
119 Scott, W. L., b. f. **Amulet**, 2, Rayon d'Or, Presto	**87**

* Declared Feb. 20, 1890.

FIFTH RACE. — For two years old. A sweepstakes of $20 each, with $1,000 added, of which $200 to second, and $100 to third. Winners of any race to carry 3 lbs. extra; of two races, 5 lbs. Beaten maidens, not having run second, allowed 5 lbs.

Six Furlongs.

SIXTH RACE. — For three years old and upward. A sweepstakes of $15 each, with $750 added, of which $100 to second, and $50 to third. WEIGHTS AT 10 LBS. BELOW THE SCALE. The winner to be sold at auction for $2,500; if entered to be sold for less, 1 lb. allowed for each $100 down to $500.

One Mile and a Furlong.

THIRD DAY.—TUESDAY, JUNE 3D.

FIRST RACE. — For maidens two years old. A sweepstakes of $20 each, with $1,000 added, of which $200 to second, and $100 to third. **Half a Mile.**

SECOND RACE.—ALGERIA HANDICAP, for three years old and upward. A sweepstakes of $30 each, or $5 if declared, with $1,500 added, of which $300 to second, and $150 to third. Entries to be made on Saturday, May 31st. Weights to be announced and declarations to be made on Monday, June 2d. **One Mile and Three Furlongs.**

THIRD RACE.—VAN NEST STAKES, for two years old. A sweepstakes of $50 each, $15 forfeit, with $1,250 added, of which $250 to second, and $100 to third. The winner to be sold at auction for $5,000. If entered by 4 p.m. on the day before the day appointed for the race to be sold for $3,000, allowed 8 lbs.; then 1 lb. for each $100 down to $2,000. Beaten horses not liable to be claimed. Closed January 2, 1890, with 101 entries. **Five Furlongs.**

1 Aby, C. W., ch. c. **Rodman,** Rutherford, Leverett.
2 Belmont, August, b. f. **Fearless,** St. Blaise, Dauntless.
3 Belmont, August, ch. g. **St. Patrick,** St. Blaise, Patience.
4 Belmont, August, ch. f. **Marigold,** St. Blaise, Simple Gold.
5 Belmont, August, ch. f. **Belligerent,** Fiddlesticks, Bellona.
6 Belmont, August, b. f. **Zenobia,** The Ill Used, Fair Barbarian.
7 Belmont, August, b. c. **Lepanto,** Kingfisher, Leightonia.
8 Beverwyck Stable, b. f. **Lottie,** Faustus, Loretto.
9 Beverwyck Stable, ch. c. **Brocker,** Faustus, Lulu.
10 Beverwyck Stable, b. f. **Polly S.,** Pizarro, Amandine.
11 Beverwyck Stable, ch. f. **Hausa,** Fellowcraft, Hanap.
12 Blunt, Edmund, b. c. **Somerset,** Stratford, Imelda.
13 Brown, S. S., b. c. ——, Richmond, Alabama.
14 Brown, S. S., ch. f. ——, Richmond, Ellen Alice.
15 Bruce, L. C., b. c. **Bryson,** Bramble, Kitty H.
16 Bruce, L. C., b. f. **Cooce,** Muscovy, Emma by Eolus.
17 Burch, W. P., ch. c. **Simon Pure,** Great Tom, Carlotta.
18 Campbell, R. E., b. f. **Saxonette,** Saxon, Marionette.
19 Castle Stable, b. c. **Homernu,** Glenelg, Return.
20 Castle Stable, ch. c. **Glideaway,** Glenelg, Schott.
21 Colaizza & Fisher, b. c. ——, Duke of Montrose, Lizzie S.
22 Conner, Wm. M., ch. c. **Glenbriar,** Glenelg, Susie Linwood.
23 Corrigan, Ed., br. f. **Corine Buckingham,** Powhattan, Hattie Harris.
24 Cotton, J., ch. c. ——, Pontiac, Lizzie Mack.
25 Daly, John, ch. f. ——, Joe Daniels, Mottle.
26 Daly, W. C., b. f. **Lizzie,** St. Blaise, Feufollet.
27 Davis & Hall, ch. c. **Vol,** Volturno, Aileen.
28 Davis & Hall, br. c. **Grapeshot,** Gaberlunzie, Fannie B.
29 Doswell, Thos. W., b. f. **Marianne,** Great Tom, Buttress.
30 Doswell, Thos. W., b. g. **Babylon,** King Bolt, Sunmaid.
31 Dwyer Bros., b. c. **Baychester,** Luke Blackburn, Silvermaid.
32 Dwyer Bros., b. c. **Great Guns,** Great Tom, Mariposa.
33 Dwyer Bros., b. c. ——, Luke Blackburn, Ogarita.

34 Dwyer Bros., b. c. **Headlight,** Hindoo, Delight.
35 Dwyer Bros., b. c. **Beware,** Billet, Distraction.
36 Dwyer Bros., ch. c. **Ourfellow,** Fellowcraft, Lena Oliver.
37 Empire Stable, ch. f. **Clover,** Milner, Fedalma.
38 Eureka Stable, b. f. **Bitter Sweet,** Bersan, Sweetheart.
39 Gideon, D., b. g. ——, Dalnacardoch, Retribution.
40 Haggin, J. B., ch. f. **Pearl Kinney,** Geo. Kinney, Pearl.
41 Haggin, J. B., ch. c. **Kilkenny,** Geo. Kinney, Bijou.
42 Hanover Stable, ch. f. ——, Neptune, Alma.
43 Hanover Stable, ch. c. ——, Spendthrift, Sinaloa.
44 Hearst, Geo., ch. c. **Anarchist,** Joe Hooker, Chestnut Bell.
45 Hearst, Geo., ch. c. **Snow Ball,** Joe Hooker, Laura Winston.
46 Hearst, Geo., ch. c. **Primero,** Powhattan, Speed.
47 Hearst, Geo., b. c. **J. B.,** Warwick, Maria F.
48 Hearst, Geo., b. c. **Yosemite,** Hyder Ali, Nellie Collier.
49 Hough Bros., ch. f. ——, Enquirer, Melita.
50 Israel, E. L., ch. f. **Harpy,** Onondaga, Flora.
51 Israel, E. L., ch. f ——, Iroquois, Valerian.
52 Jennings, W. B., b. f. ——, Onondaga, Kelp.
53 Jennings, Wm., b. f. **Antelope,** Tom Ochiltree, Slipper Dance.
54 Lakeland, Wm., br. c. **Willie L.,** Falsetto, Miranda.
55 Leach, Geo. T., blk. c. ——, Vocalic, Frances L.
56 Littlefield, C., ch. c. **Simrock,** Fellowcraft, Almira.
57 McClelland, Byron, ch. c. **Outcry,** Blue Eyes, Etna.
58 McElmeel, E., ch. c. ——, Bend'Or, Eusebia.
59 McMahon & Co., ch. f. **Emma J.,** Stratford, Roulette.
60 Madison Stable, ch. g. **Austral,** Reform, Australind.
61 Madison Stable, b. f. **Penitent,** Pardee, Essayez II.
62 Madison Stable, br. f. **Bonita,** Dalnacardoch, Preciosa.
63 Maxwell, Clark, b. c. **Volo,** Voltigeur, Clara B.
64 Morris, G. B., b. c. **Lawrence,** Longfellow, Miss Lawrence.
65 Morris, J. A. & A. H., br. f. **Zulu,** Pizarro, Zoo Zoo.
66 Morris, J. A. & A. H., b. c. **Chatham,** St. Blaise, Clara.
67 Morris, J. A. & A. H., b. c. **Terrifier,** Alarm, Bonnella.
68 Morris, J. A. & A. H., br. f. imp. **Serene,** Sterling, Sedate.
69 Morris, J. A. & A. H., b. f. **Highland Lass,** Pizarro, Belle of the High-
 lands.
70 Morris, J. A. & A. H., ch. f. **Glucose,** Kyrle Daly, Mura.
71 Morris, J. A. & A. H., b. f. **Truth,** Rotherhill or Bersan, Virtue.
72 Morris, J. A. & A. H., ch. c. **Affection,** St. Blaise, Affinity.
73 Morris, J. A. & A. H., b. c. **Hands Off,** Luke Blackburn, Touch-me-not.
74 Palo Alto S. F., ch. c. **Rinfax,** Argyle, Amelia.
75 Preakness Stable, ch. f. **Adelina,** Macduff, Adele.
76 Pulsifer, D. T., ch. c. **Sir George,** Spendthrift, Piccadilly.
77 Pulsifer, D. T., ch. c. **Judge Mitchell,** Stratford, Heatherbelle.
78 Pulsifer, D. T., b. c. **Kirkover,** Atilla, The Squaw.
79 Rancocas Stable, br. c. **Cyrus,** Emperor, Cyrilla.
80 Rancocas Stable, b. c. **Sirocco,** Emperor, Breeze.
81 Rancocas Stable, br. c. **Happy Day,** Emperor, Felicity.
82 Rancocas Stable, b. f. **Vanity,** Rotherhill or Glenelg, Pride.
83 Rancocas Stable, b. f. **Arrogance,** Emperor, Disdain.
84 Reed, Chas. & Sons, ch. c. **Benjamin,** Mr. Pickwick, Countess.
85 Reed, Chas. & Sons, ch. c. **Patrick,** Mr. Pickwick, Queen of Hearts.
86 Reed, Chas. & Sons, ch. c. **Peter,** Long Taw, Athlene.
87 Riley, B., br. f. **Seabird,** Sensation, Fiona.
88 Rose, L. J., b. c. **Mas Rico,** Shannon, Fannie Lewis.
89 Sands, Wm. H., b. c. ——, Kyrle Daly, Trellis.
90 Santa Anita Stable, ch. c. **El Carman,** Gano, Grey Anne.
91 Scott, W. L., ch. f. **Cutalong,** Rayon d'Or, Claudia.
92 Scott, W. L., br. f. **Wendaway,** Wanderer, Waitaway.
93 Scott, W. L., b. g. **Tourist,** Wanderer, Bordelaise.
94 Scott, W. L., ch. c. **Rushlight,** Wanderer, Blue Cap.
95 Scott, W. L., b. f. **Fugitive,** Wanderer, Honey Bee.
96 Street, S. W., ch. c. **Outcome,** Forester, Income.
97 Walden, Jeter, ch. c. **Combustion,** Geo. Kinney, Naptha.

(23)

98 Warnke, H. & Son, ch. c. **Forward**, Farandole, Tambourine.
99 Warnke, H. & Son, ch. c. **King Iro**, Iroquois, Tallulah.
100 Warnke, H. & Son, ch. f. **Clara Lee**, Great Tom, Clara L.
101 Warnke, H. & Son, b. f. **Ella T.**, Himyar, Ella G.

To be run under the auspices of the American Jockey Club.

FOURTH RACE. — LADIES' STAKES, for fillies three years old. A sweepstakes of $100 each, h.f., or $20 if declared by July 1, 1889, with $1,500 added, of which $250 to second, and $100 to third. Winners in 1890 of $1,500 to carry 3 lbs.; of two such races, or one of $3,000, 6 lbs.; of two of $3,000, 9 lbs. extra. Non-winners of a sweepstakes for three years old allowed 5 lbs. Maidens allowed 10 lbs. Closed August 15, 1888, with 99 entries.

1,400 Yards.

Old Scale of Weight.

1 Auburndale Stable, ch. f. **Unadaga**, Onondaga, Una.
2 Auburndale Stable, b. f. **Folly**, Onondaga, Paradox.
3 Bathgate, Chas. W., b. f. ——, Lyttleton, Mystification.
4 Bell & Timberlake (Melbourne Stable), b. f. **Blue Vail**, Billet, Juanita.
5 Belmont, August, ch. f. **Her Highness**, St. Blaise, Princess.
6 Belmont, August, ch. f. **Phoebe**, St. Blaise, Mehallah.†
7 Belmont, August, ch. f. **Faustina**, St. Blaise, Farina.*
8 Belmont, August, ch. f. **Cara Mia**, St. Blaise, Carita.*
9 Belmont, August, b. f. **Amazon**, The Ill Used, Fair Barbarian.
10 Belmont, August, b. f. **Tomboy**, The Ill Used, Madcap.†
11 Belmont, August, b. f. **Cornelia**, The Ill Used, Cordelia.
12 Belmont, August, b. f. **Leda**, Kingfisher, Leightonia.
13 Bowie, Oden, b. f. **Alarm Bell**, Alarm, Belle Meade.
14 Bowie, Oden, ch. f. **Fairy**, Vassal, Fairview.
15 Breeze Hill Stock Farm, blk. f. **Miss de Cornis**, Keene Richards Jr., Maggie B.
16 Breeze Hill Stock Farm, b. f. **Mazie**, Keene Richards Jr., Reata.
17 Castle Stable, b. or br. f. ——, Iroquois, Explosion.
18 Castle Stable, b. f. ——, Warwick or Sir Modred, Nellie Peyton.
19 Castle Stable, br. f. ——, Dalnacardoch, Yorkshire Lass.
20 Clay, T. J., b. f. **Ballyhoo**, Duke of Magenta, Baby.*
21 Clay, T. J., br. f. **Escapade**, Onondaga, Hypatia.*
22 Conner, Wm. M., ch. f. **Beatify**, Onondaga, Bliss.
23 Conner, Wm. M., ch. f. **Tampette**, Dalnacardoch, Waltz.
24 Conner, Wm. M., br. f. **Galliard**, Reform. Glidelia.
25 Conner, Wm. M., b. f. **Chimere**, Iroquois, Chimera.
26 Conner, Wm. M. (Melbourne Stable), ch. f. **Racemede**, Hindoo, Calomel.*
27 Corrigan, P., ch. f. **Purity**, Hindoo, Eppie L.*
28 Cotton & Boyle, ch. f. ——, Kyrle Daly, Assyria.
29 Cotton & Boyle, blk. f. ——, Kyrle Daly, Elizabeth.
30 Cotton & Boyle, b. f. ——, Sir Modred or Kyrle Daly, Rosemary.
31 Cotton & Boyle, b. f. ——, Kyrle Daly, Comanche.
32 Crawford & Roche, b. f. **Alby**, Glengarry, Dublin Belle.
33 Davidson, J. H. (Melbourne Stable), b. f. **Trinity**, King Alfonso, Vendu.
34 Davis & Hall, br. f. ——, Iroquois, Cyrilla.
35 Davis & Hall, b. f. **Little Ella**, Little Phil, Ella Warfield.
36 Dwyer Bros., b. f. **Blue Dress**, Enquirer, Bribery.
37 Dwyer Bros., b. f. **Red Dress**. King Alfonso, Lilly Duke.
38 Dwyer Bros., b. f. ——, Glengarry, Hop.*
39 Dwyer Bros., b. f. ——, Enquirer, Colossa.
40 Flynn, J. (Melbourne Stable), b. f. **Gilgal**, Billet, Miss Annie.
41 Gideon, D. (John D. Morrissey), ch. f. **Bennett**, Spendthrift, Phœbe Mayflower.†

(24)

42 Hearst, Geo., b. f. **Golden Horn**, Spendthrift, Constantinople.
43 Hearst, Geo., b. f. **Gloaming**, Sir Modred, Twilight.
44 Hearst, Geo., o. f. ———, Warwick, Mileta.
45 Hearst, Geo., blk. f. **Everglade**, Iroquois, Agenoria.
46 Hearst, Geo., ch. f. ———, Warwick, Cinderella.
47 Jennings, W. B., b. f. ———, Billet, Weiland.*
48 Lorillard, L. L., b. f. **Sif**, Pizarro, Susan Ann.
49 McCarty, D. J. & Bro. (W. L. Scott), ch. f. **Pandora**, Rayon d'Or, Blue Grass Belle.
50 McElmeel, E., b. or br. f. ———, General Monroe, Aline.
51 Madison Stable, b. f. **Laurentia**, Fiddlesticks or Kingfisher or St. Blaise, Laurette.†
52 Madison Stable, b. f. **Tocsin**, Alarm, Auricula.*
53 Madison Stable, b. f. **Sonora**, Spendthrift, Sinaloa.*
54 Madison Stable, ch. f. **Ballad**, Greenland, Sonnet.*
55 Maltese Villa Stock Farm, ch. f. **Mirope**, Joe Hooker, Constellation.*
56 Miller, J. Henry (Melbourne Stable), ch. f. **Intrepid**, Hindoo, Jaconet.*
57 Morris, G. B. (Melbourne Stable), b. f. **The Tigress**, Billet, Vega.*
58 Morris, J. A. & A. H., ch. f. **Constellation**, Tom Ochiltree, Minnie Mc.*
59 Morris, J. A. & A. H., ch. f. **Ambition**, Tom Ochiltree, Aspiration.*
60 Morris, J. A. & A. H., ch. f. **Homœopathy**, Reform, Maggie B. B.
61 Morris, J. A. & A. H., ch. f. **Winsome**, Kyrle Daly, Winnifred.*
62 Morris, J. A. & A. H., b. f. **Starlight**, Iroquois, Vandalite.
63 Morris, J. A. & A. H., b. f. **Lady McNairy**, Duke of Magenta, Sudie McNairy.
64 Morris, J. A. & A. H., b. or br. f. **Despair**, Falsetto, Desolation.*
65 Morris, J. A. & A H., b. f. **Chemistry**, Longfellow, Lenore.*
66 Morris, J. A. & A. H., ch. f. ———, Hindoo, Mattie Amelia.
67 Morris, J. A. & A. H., b. f. **Queen Little**, King Ernest, Minority.*
68 Murphy, Dennis (Madison Stable), b. or br. f. **Vera**, Greenland, Maggie J.†
69 Murphy, Dennis (Madison Stable), ch. c. **Ganador**, Greenland, Patti.‡
70 Oakwood Stable, b. f. ———, Long Taw, Helen.
71 Oakwood Stable, ch. f. ———, Bramble or Geo. Kinney, Decoy Duck.
72 Oakwood Stable, blk. or br. f. ———, Hindoo, Mary B.
73 Oakwood Stable, br. f. ———, Stratford, Lolah.
74 O'Brien, Dan, ch. f. **Sister Geneva**, King Ban, Buff and Blue.
75 Pincus, J., ch. f. ———, King Ban, Flora.
76 Preakness Stable, b. f. **Fidelio**, Falsetto, Gleam.
77 Preakness Stable, br. f. **Livonia**, Longfellow, Elkhorn Lass.
78 Ramapo Stable, br. f. ———, Runnymede, Giroflé.
79 Santa Anita Stable, ch. f. **Sinaloa II.**, Grinstead, Maggie Emerson.
80 Santa Anita Stable, ch. f. **Violette**, Grinstead, Hermosa.
81 Santa Anita Stable, ch. f. **St. Cecilia**, Grinstead, Sister Anne.
82 Santa Anita Stable, b. f. **Atlanta**, Grinstead, Blossom.
83 Santa Anita Stable, ch. f. **Orange Leaf**, Rutherford, Fallen Leaf.
84 Santa Anita Stable, b. f. ———, Glenelg, Malta.
85 Scott, W. L., ch. f. **Paradox**, Rayon d'Or, Lizzie Cox.
86 Scott, W. L., ch. f. **Minuet**, Rayon d'Or, Reel Dance.
87 Scott, W. L., ch. f. **Martha**, Rayon d'Or, Lucy Wallace.
88 Scott, W. L., b. f. **Runaway**, Algerine, Belle of Eltham.*
89 Scott, W. L., ch. f. **Laura**, Algerine, Grey Gown.
90 Scott, W. L., b. f. **Hebe**, Kantaka, Mary Constant.*
91 Stevens, T. H., ch. f. ———, Onondaga, Square Dance.
92 Tucker, R., ch. f. **Millie Williams**, Glengarry, Arizona.*
93 Tucker, R., b. f. **Pinkie J.**, Glengarry, Azalia.*
94 Westbury Stable, ch. f. **Caress**, Woodlands, Inka.
95 Withers, D. D., b. f. ———, Uncas, Faverdale.
96 Withers, D. D., b. f. ———, King Ernest, Invermore.
97 Withers, D. D., ch. f. ———, King Ernest, Knicknack.
98 Withers, D. D., ch. f. ———, †Kinglike, Miss Bassett.
99 Withers, D. D., ch. f. ———, Kinglike, Revolt.

* Declared July 1st, 1889.   † Declared since July 1st, 1889.   ‡ Void.

FIFTH RACE. — For all ages. A sweepstakes of $15 each, with $750 added, of which $100 to second, and $50 to third. The winner to be sold at auction for $2,500; if entered to be sold for less, 1 lb. allowed for each $100 down to $500.

Seven Furlongs.

SIXTH RACE. — For three years old and upward. A sweepstakes of $15 each, with $750 added, of which $100 to second, and $50 to third. Winners in 1889 or 1890 of $2,000 to carry 5 lbs. extra; twice of $2,000, or once of $5,000, 7 lbs. extra. Non-winners in 1889 or 1890 of $1,000 allowed 7 lbs. Beaten maidens allowed 12 lbs.

One Mile.

FOURTH DAY.—WEDNESDAY, JUNE 4TH.

FIRST RACE. — For all ages. A sweepstakes of $15 each, with $750 added, of which $100 to second, and $50 to third. The winner of the opening scramble to carry 5 lbs. extra.

Six Furlongs.

SECOND RACE. — SAN SIMEON HANDICAP, for three years old and upward. A sweepstakes of $20 each, or $5 if declared, with $1,000 added, of which $200 to second, and $100 to third. Entries to be made on Monday, June 2. Weights to be announced and declarations to be made on Tuesday, June 3.

One Mile and a Furlong.

To be run under the auspices of the American Jockey Club.

THIRD RACE. — JUVENILE STAKES, for two years old. A sweepstakes of $50 each, h.f., or only $10 if declared by January 1, 1890, with $1,500 added, of which $250 to second. Winners of $5,000 to carry 5 lbs.; of $10,000, 7 lbs. extra. Closed August 15, 1889, with 63 entries.   **Half a Mile.**

1 Auburndale Stable, br. c. **St. Crescent,** St. Blaise, Lorelle.
2 Auburndale Stable, ch. f. ——, Onondaga, Gleam.
3 Belmont, August, b. c. **Lepanto,** Kingfisher, Leightonia.
4 Belmont, August, ch. c. **St. Charles,** St Blaise, Carita.
5 Belmont, August, ch. c. **St. Omer,** St. Blaise, Olitipa.*
6 Belmont, August, ch. c. **Jack of Diamonds,** St. Blaise, Nellie James.
7 Blunt, Edmund C., b. c. **Somerset,** Stratford, Imelda.
8 Blunt, Edmund C., b. f. **Hari Kari,** Macaroon, Herodia.
9 Brown, S. S., ch. c. ——, Richmond, Mayfield.
10 Brown, S. S., ch. c. ——, Richmond, La Cigale.*
11 Brown, S. S., b. c. ——, Richmond, Alabama.*
12 Brown, S. S., ch. c. ——, Richmond, Gladys.
13 Bruce, L. C., ch. c. **Brentano,** Great Tom, Addie Hart.
14 Bruce, L. C., b. f. **Krikina,** Muscovy, Krik.
15 Cotton, J., ch. c. ——, Pontiac. Lizzie Mack.
16 Daly, Marcus, ch. c. ——, Sir Modred, Trade Dollar.
17 Daly, Marcus, b. c. ——, Sir Modred, Carissima.
18 Daly, Marcus, br. c. ——, Darebin, Agenoria.*
19 Daly, Marcus, ch. c. ——, St. Blaise, Maud Hampton.
20 Daly, Marcus, b. c. ——, Ban Fox, Queen.
21 Daly, Marcus, b. c. ——, John Happy, Susan.*
22 Daly, W. C., ch. f. ——, St. Blaise, Feufollet.
23 Daly, W. C., br. f. ——, St. Blaise, Felicia.
24 Davis & Hall, ch. c. ——, Luke Blackburn, Janet Norton.
25 Davis & Hall, ch. f. ——, Gaberlunzie, Eunice.
26 Dwyer Bros., b. c. **Baychester,** Luke Blackburn, Silvermaid.
27 Dwyer Bros., b. c. **Great Guns,** Great Tom, Mariposa.
28 Dwyer Bros., b. c. **Beware,** Billet, Distraction.
29 Dwyer Bros., b. or br. f. ——, Hindoo, Bourbon Belle.
30 Dwyer Bros., blk. f. ——, Hindoo, Katie.
31 Dwyer Bros., ch. c. **Young George,** Geo. Kinney, Arizona.

(27)

Fourth Day. — Wednesday, June 4th.

32 Empire Stable, b. c. **Lyceum**, Prince of Norfolk, Sister to Jim Douglass.
33 Empire Stable, ch. f. **Landscape**, Woodlands, Artifice.
34 Excelsior Stable, br. c. ——, Reform, Zicka.
35 Excelsior Stable, b. c. ——, Sir Modred, Yolande.
36 Gray & Co., b. c. **Zender**, Faustus, Bank Stock.
37 Gray & Co., ch. c. **Ketchum**, Faustus, Anna Richards.
38 Hogan, M., ch. f. **Maggie Ward**, Luke Blackburn, Baby Blake.
39 Hogan, M., b. c. **F. D. Ward**. Bramble, Bobinet.
40 Hunter, John, ch. or rn. c. **Conundrum**, Enquirer, Tassel.
41 Hunter, John, ch. c. **Tantrum**, Great Tom, Mozelle.
42 Hunter, John, ch. c. **Calcium**, Great Tom, Bonnie Belle.
43 Hunter, John, ch. c. **Orawampum**, Onondaga, Nellie Booker.
44 Hunter, John, b. c. **Dictum**, Iroquois, Bonnie Meade.
45 Hunter, John, b. c. **Humdrum**, Warwick, Wild Rose.
46 Hunter, John, ch. c. **Hoodlum**, Joe Daniels, Miss Clay.
47 Hunter, John, b. c. **Kiawah**, Iroquois, Buttercup.
48 Kraus, Geo. J., b. c. **Happy George**, John Happy, Florine.
49 Ramapo Stable, blk. f. ——, Iroquois, Planchette.
50 Ramapo Stable, b. f. ——, Kingfisher, Genevra.
51 Rancocas Stable, b. c. **Sirocco**, Emperor, Breeze.
52 Rancocas Stable, b. f. **Pandora**, Emperor, Susan Ann.*
53 Rancocas Stable, ch. f. **Portia**, Joe Daniels, Sly Dance.*
54 Rancocas Stable, br. f. **Morgheda**, Iroquois, Marchioness.*
55 Rancocas Stable, b. f. **Vanity**, Rotherhill or Glenelg, Pride.
56 Rancocas Stable, br. c. **Happy Day**, Emperor, Felicity.
57 Sands, W. H., b. c. ——, Kyrle Daly, Trellis.
58 Scott, W. L., b. f. **Wendaway**, Wanderer, Waitaway.
59 Scott, W. L., ch. f. **Sea Shore**, Wanderer, Lison.
60 Scott, W. L., b. f. **Maywood**, Rayon d'Or, Belle of Maywood.
61 Scott, W. L., ch. f. **Turmoil**, Rayon d'Or, Lilly R.
62 Street, S. W., ch. c. **Bourgham**, Kantaka, Ione.
63 Wood, W. G., b. c. **King Silver**, Silver Mine, Miss Mickey.

*Declared January 1st, 1890.

FOURTH RACE. — FLEETWOOD STAKES, for three years old. A sweepstakes of $100 each, h.f., or only $20 if declared by January 1, 1890, with $2,000 added, of which $500 to second, and $200 to third.   Closed August 15, 1889, with 74 entries.   **One Mile.**

1 Auburndale Stable, ch. c. **King Hazem**, King Ban, Hazem.
2 Auburndale Stable, ch. g. ——, Harry O'Fallon, Sue Finnie.
3 Belmont, August, ch. c. **Chesapeake**, St. Blaise, Susquehanna.
4 Belmont, August, ch. c. **St. Carlo**, St. Blaise, Carina.
5 Belmont, August, ch. c. **Padishah**, St. Blaise, Sultana.
6 Belmont, August, b. c. **Magnate**, The Ill Used, Magnetism.
7 Belmont, August, b. c. **Lord Dalmeny**, The Ill Used, Lady Rosebery.*
8 Brown, Ed., b. c. **Prodigal Son**, Pat Malloy, Homeward Bound.
9 Brown, Ed., b. f. **Charming**, Prince Charlie, Nannie Bay.
10 Brown, Ed., b. f. **Ruperta**, Prince Charlie, Marguerite.
11 Brown, Ed., b. f. **Pearl Set**, Falsetto, Pearl Thorn.
12 Brown, S. S., b. c. ——, Powhattan, Lady Jane.
13 Brown, S. S., b. c. ——, Leonatus, Martina.
14 Brown, S. S., b. c. ——, Ten Broeck, Belle of Nantura.
15 Brown, S. S., b. c. ——, Longfellow, Rosemary.
16 Brown, S. S., b. g. ——, Longfellow, Anne Boleyn.
17 Brown, S. S., b. c. ——, Geo. Kinney, Matinee.
18 Beverwyck Stable, b. f. **Minuet**, Glenelg, La Polka.
19 Beverwyck Stable, ch. f. **Can Can**, Prince Charlie, La Esmeralda.
20 Campbell, R. E., b. c. **Protection**, Prince Charlie, Manola.

(28)

21 Castle Stable, ch. c. **Elkton**, Eolus, Helen.
22 Castle Stable, br. c. **Elmstone**, Stonehenge, Majority.
23 Chicago Stable, br. c. **Robespierre**, Jils Johnson, Agnes.
24 Davis & Hall, b. c. **Fad**, Fadladeen, Betsy.
25 Davis & Hall, b. f. **Little Ella**, Little Phil, Ella Warfield.
26 Dwyer Bros., b. c. **Blackburn**, Luke Blackburn, Tomboy.
27 Dwyer Bros., ch. c. **Caldwell**, Ten Broeck, Miss Nailor.
28 Dwyer Bros., b. c. **June Day**, Falsetto, Virga.
29 Dwyer Bros., b. c. **Flatbush**, Glenelg, Florida.
30 Dwyer Bros., b. c. **Houston**, Hindoo, Bourbon Belle.
31 Dwyer Bros., b. c. **Bluebird**, Billet, Mundane.
32 Dwyer Bros., b. c. **Extra Dry**, Glenelg, Peru.
33 Dwyer Bros., b. c. **Longford**, Longfellow, Semper Idem.
34 Empire Stable, b. c. **Favorite**, Fiddlesticks, Favonia.
35 Gray & Co., b. c. **Roseberry**, Faustus, Bonnie Rose.
36 Hannigan, John & Co., b. c. **Milldale**, Onondaga, Emily F.
37 Hearst, Geo., b. c. **King Thomas**, King Ban, Maud Hampton.
38 Hearst, Geo., b. c. **Ballarat**, Sir Modred, La Favorita.
39 Hearst, Geo., b. c. **Anaconda**, Spendthrift, Maid of Athol.
40 Hearst, Geo., br. c. **Tournament**, Sir Modred, Plaything.
41 Hearst, Geo., b. f. **Gloaming**, Sir Modred, Twilight.
42 Hearst, Geo., b. f. **Golden Horn**, Spendthrift, Constantinople.
43 Hearst, Geo., blk. f. **Everglade**, Iroquois, Agenoria.
44 Hough Bros., b. c. **Drizzle**, Ventilator, Mag.
45 McGuigan, A., b. c. **Queer Toy**, Enquirer, Toilet.*
46 McMahon, Wm. (A. J. Cassatt), br. c. **Eurochlydon**, Eolus, Majestic.
47 Madison Stable, b. c. **Devotee**, Alarm, Sister of Mercy.
48 Madison Stable, b. c. **Iago**, Bend'Or, Billetdoux.
49 Madison Stable, b. c. **Austalitz**, Greenland, Australina.*
50 Maltese Villa Stock Farm, b. c. **Abdiel**, Jocko, Cousin Peggy.
51 Morris, G. B., ch. c. **Jersey Pat**, Pat Malloy, Jersey Lass.
52 Morris, G. B., b. c. **Lisimony**, Lisbon, Patrimony.
53 Morris, J. A. & A. H., ch. c. **Cayuga**, Iroquois, Letola.
54 Morris, J. A. & A. H., b. c. **Civil Service**, Reform, Bonnella.*
55 Morris, J. A. & A. H., br. c. **Mucilage**, Kyrle Daly, Mura.*
56 Morris, J. A. & A. H., br. c. **Dr. Helmuth**, Sir Modred, Sweetbriar.
57 Morris, J. A. & A. H., ch. f. **Druidess**, Stonehenge, Castagnette.
58 Morris, J. A. & A. H., ch. f. **Homœopathy**, Reform, Maggie B. B.
59 Morris, J. A. & A. H., br. f. **Starlight**, Iroquois, Vandalite.
60 Morris, J. A. & A. H., b. f. **Frailty**, Prince Charlie, Blunder.*
61 Preakness Stable, b. c. **Windsor**, Sir Modred or Warwick, Lady Middleton.*
62 Preakness Stable, b. c. **Monroe**, Macduff, Bonnie Lizzie.
63 Sands, Wm. H., br. c. **Heathen**, Hindoo, Jennie Blue.
64 Scott, A. J., b. g. **Gunwad**, Gunnar, Annie S.
65 Scott, W. L., ch. c. **Leighton**, Rayon d'Or, L'Argentine.
66 Scott, W. L., b. g. **Banquet**, Rayon d'Or, Ella T.
67 Scott, W. L., ch. c. **Torso**, Algerine, Santa Lucia.
68 Scott, W. L., ch. g. **Chaos**, Rayon d'Or, Lilly R.
69 Shippee, L. M., b. c. **Fellowcharm**, Longfellow, Trinket.
70 Stanley, F. G., blk. c. **Onaway**, Onondaga, Kelp.
71 Stanley, F. G., blk. c. **Ralph Bayard**, Muscovy, Imperatrice.
72 Withers, D. D., b. c. ——, Stonehenge, Eccola.
73 Withers, D. D., b. c. ——, Kinglike, Fanfan.
74 Withers, D. D., b. c. ——, King Ernest, Cyclone.

* Declared January 1st, 1890.

FIFTH RACE. — For fillies two years old. A sweepstakes of
$20 each, with $1,000 added, of which $200 to second, and $100 to
third. Non-winners of $1,000 allowed 7 lbs. Beaten maidens
allowed 12 lbs. **Five Furlongs.**

SIXTH RACE. — For three years old and upward. A sweepstakes of $15 each, with $750 added, of which $100 to second, and
$50 to third. The winner to be sold at auction for $5,000; if entered to be sold for $4,000, allowed 5 lbs.; if for $3,000, 12 lbs.; if
for $2,000, 20 lbs. **One Mile and a Furlong.**

FIFTH DAY.—THURSDAY, JUNE 5TH.

FIRST RACE. — For two years old that have never started. A sweepstakes of $20 each, with $1,000 added, of which $200 to second, and $100 to third.　**Five Furlongs.**

SECOND RACE.—RANCOCAS HANDICAP, for three years old and upward. A sweepstakes of $30 each, or $5 if declared, with $1,500 added, of which $300 to second, and $150 to third. Entries to be made on Tuesday, June 3. Weights to be announced and declarations to be made on Wednesday, June 4.
One Mile and Five Furlongs.

THIRD RACE.—CASANOVA STAKES, for fillies two years old. A sweepstakes of $100 each, h.f., or only $20 if declared by April 1, with $2,000 added, of which $500 to second, and $200 to third. Winners of a race of $3,000, or of two of $2,000, to carry 5 lbs. extra. Beaten maidens allowed 5 lbs. Closed January 2, 1890, with 92 entries.　**Six Furlongs.**

1 Auburndale Stable, ch. f. ——, Onondaga, Gleam.
2 Barbee, Geo., ch. f., **Coquette,** Fonso, Ardente.
3 Belmont, August, ch. f. **La Tosca,** St. Blaise, Toucques.
4 Belmont, August, ch. f. **Beauty,** St. Blaise, Bella.
5 Belmont, August, ch. f. **Flavia,** St. Blaise, Flavina.
6 Belmont, August, ch. f. **Belligerent,** Fiddlesticks, Bellona.
7 Beverwyck Stable, b. f. **Bertha Campbell,** King Alfonso, Vulpine.
8 Beverwyck Stable, b. f. **Polly S.,** Pizarro, Amandine.
9 Beverwyck Stable, ch. f. **Hansa,** Fellowcraft, Hanap.
10 Brown, S. S., ch. f. ——, Himyar, Jewel.
11 Brown, S. S., ch. f. ——, Richmond, Ellen Alice.
12 Bruce, L. C., br. f. **Vocaletta,** Vocalic, Vietta.
13 Bruce, L. C., b. f. **Krikina,** Muscovy, Krik.
14 Clover Stable, br. f. **Margherita,** Rossifer, Certiorari.
15 Clover Stable, ch. f. **Sarah Hall,** Stratford, Minnie Andrews.
16 Conner, Wm. M., ch. f. **Furlano,** Woodlands, Waltz.
17 Conner, Wm. M., ch. f. **Gardelia,** Woodlands, Glidelia.
18 Conner, Wm. M., b. f. **Imperieuse,** Pizarro, Imogene.
19 Conner Wm. M., br. f. **Beata,** Strathmore, Beatrice.
20 Corrigan, Ed., br. f. **Corine Buckingham,** Powhattan, Hattie Harris.
21 Daly, Marcus, ch. f. **Bonnie Lass.** Sir Modred, Bonnie Kate.
22 Daly, Marcus, ch. f. **Leonora,** Sir Modred, Lizzie Lucas.
23 Daly, Marcus, b. f. **Mistletoe,** Sir Modred, Letola.
24 Daly, Marcus, b. f. **Namouna,** Sir Modred, La Favorita.
25 Davis & Hall, ch. f. **Euna,** Gaberlunzie, Eunice.
26 Davis & Hall, b. f. **Gaiety,** Gaberlunzie, Kenita.
27 Dwyer Bros., blk. f. ——, Hindoo, Katie.
28 Dwyer Bros., b. f. ——, Hindoo, Bourbon Belle.
29 Dwyer Bros., ch. f. **Ada C.,** Himyar, Fannie.
30 Empire Stable, ch. f. **Landscape,** Woodlands, Artifice.
31 Empire Stable, br. f. **Calypso,** St. Blaise, Carmen.
32 Gray & Co., b. f. **Betty Prather.** Faustus, Zula.
33 Greener, Jno. G., ch. f. **Eugenie,** Enquirer, Miss Harding.

34 Hearst, Geo., blk. f. **Firework,** Falsetto, Explosion.
35 Hearst, Geo., ch. f. **Babicora,** Hyder Ali, Graciosa.
36 Hough Bros., ch. f. ———, Enquirer, Melita.
37 Hough Bros., b. f. **Queer Girl,** Himyar, Queen Ban.
38 Hunter, John, blk. f. **Ontawin,** Onondaga, Annette.
39 Hunter, John, b. f. **Mayflower,** Iroquois, Blue Gown.
40 Israel, E. L., ch. f. **Harpy,** Onondaga, Flora.
41 Israel, E. L. ch. f. ———, Iroquois, Valerian.
42 Kernoghan, G. H., br. f. **Dodo,** Falsetto, Brocade.
43 Kernoghan, G. H., b. f. ———, Duke of Montrose, Helen Wallace.
44 Kneale, James, b. f. **Miss Williams,** Himyar, Grace Lee.
45 Littlefield, C., b. f. **Miss Himyar,** Himyar, Dixietta.
46 McClelland, Byron, ch. f. **Sallie McClelland,** Hindoo, Red and Blue.
47 McClelland, Byron, br. f. ———, Billet, Retreat.
48 McElmeel, E., b. f. ———, Stratford, Manmee.
49 Maltese Villa, S. F., br. f. **Romcetta,** Woodlands, Dizzy Blonde.
50 Morris, J. A. & A. H., br. f. **Ambulance,** Onondaga, Black Maria.
51 Morris, J. A. & A. H., b. f. **Persistence,** Sir Modred, Parthenia.
52 Morris, J. A. & A. H., ch. f. **Reckon,** Pizarro, Perhaps.
53 Morris, J. A. & A. H., b. f. **Vacation,** Tom Ochiltree, Minnie Mc.
54 Morris, J. A. & A. H., b. f. **Correction,** Himyar, Mannie Gray.
55 Morris, J. A. & A. H., b. f. **Truth,** Rotherhill or Bersan, Virtue.
56 Morris, J. A. & A. H., ch. f. **Affection,** St. Blaise, Affinity.
57 Morris, J. A. & A. H., b. f. **Compassion,** Alarm, Sister of Mercy.
58 Morris, J. A. & A. H., ch. f. imp. **Prosperity,** Zealot, Wealth.
59 New York Stable, ch. f. **Mauve,** Fonso, Mabille.
60 Palo Alto S. F., ch. f. **Tearless,** Wildidle, Teardrop.
61 Palo Alto S. F., ch. f. **Rosebud,** Wildidle, Rosetta.
62 Preakness Stable, b. f. **Lizzette,** Hindoo, Bonnie Lizzie.
63 Preakness Stable, ch. f. **Flavilla,** Macduff, Vintage.
64 Ramapo Stable, br. f. ———, Iroquois, Guildean.
65 Rancocas Stable, b. f. **Vanity,** Rotherhill or Glenelg, Pride.
66 Rancocas Stable, ch. f. **Lima,** Pizarro, Gladiola.
67 Rancocas Stable, b. f. **Arrogance,** Emperor, Disdain.
68 Rollins, W. C., b. f. ———, Gunnar, Annie S.
69 Rollins, W. C., b. f. ———, Hock Hocking, Maid of the Mist.
70 Rose, L. J., b. f. **Fury,** Argyle, Fairy Rose.
71 Santa Anita Stable, b. f. **Esperanza,** Grinstead, Hermosa.
72 Santa Anita Stable, b. f. **Cleopatra,** Grinstead, Maggie Emerson.
73 Santa Anita Stable, b. f. **Ogarita,** Longfellow, Mission Belle.
74 Santa Anita Stable, b. f. **Lacienga,** Grinstead, Jennie D.
75 Scott, W. L., br. f. **Amulet,** Rayon d'Or, Presto.
76 Scott, W. L., ch. f. **Miss Ransom,** Rayon d'Or, Nellie Ransom.
77 Scott, W. L., b. f. **Maywood,** Rayon d'Or, Belle of Maywood.
78 Scott, W. L., ch. f. **Turmoil,** Rayon d'Or, Lilly R.
79 Scott, W. L., b. f. **Exclusion,** Rayon d'Or, Monopoly.
80 Scott, W. L., ch. f. **Millrace,** Wanderer, Santa Lucia.
81 Scott, W. L., b. f. **Tudie,** Wanderer, Clemency.
82 Scott, W. L., ch. f. **Seashore,** Wanderer, Lison.
83 Shippee, L. U., b. f. **May H.,** Falsetto, Glenluine.
84 Shippee. L. U., b. f. **False Queen,** Falsetto, Queen Victoria.
85 Street, S. W., br. f. **Aunt Emma,** Spendthrift, Maid of Athol.
86 Stuart, Louis & Co., b. f. ———, Mr. Pickwick, Acquittal.
87 Union Stable, ch. f. **Polydora,** St. Blaise, Polenta.
88 Walbaum, G., b. f. **Miss Winkle,** Fellowcraft, Lady in Waiting.
89 Walden, Jeter, br. f. **Katrina,** Kyrle Daly or Sir Modred, Miss Laura.
90 Walden, Jeter, blk. f. **Favora,** Himyar, Favoress.
91 Warnke, H. & Son, ch. f. **Clara Lee,** Great Tom, Clara L.
92 Warnke, H. & Son, b. f. **Ella T.,** Himyar, Ella G.

FOURTH RACE. — ELMS STAKES, for fillies three years

old. A sweepstakes of $100 each, h.f., or only $20 if declared by January 1st, 1890, with $2,000 added, of which $500 to second, and $200 to third. Non-winners in 1890 of $2,000 (handicaps not counting), allowed 5 lbs. Beaten maidens allowed 10 lbs. Closed August 15th, 1889, with 47 entries.

One Mile and a Furlong.

1 Auburndale Stable, ch. f. **Unadaga**, Onondaga, Una.
2 Auburndale Stable, b. f. **Folly**, Onondaga, Paradox.
3 Belmont, August, ch. f. **Her Highness**, St. Blaise, Princess.*
4 Belmont, August, b. f. **Leda**, Kingfisher, Leightonia.
5 Belmont, August, b. f. **Amazon**, The Ill Used, Fair Barbarian.
6 Brown, Ed., b. f. **Charming**, Prince Charlie, Nannie Bay.
7 Brown, Ed., b. f. **Ruperta**, Prince Charlie, Marguerite.
8 Brown, Ed., b. f. **Pearl Set**, Falsetto, Pearl Thorn.
9 Brown, S. S., gr. f. ——, Springbok, Jennie V.
10 Beverwyck Stable, b. f. **Minuet**, Glenelg, La Polka.
11 Beverwyck Stable, ch. f. **Can Can**, Prince Charlie, La Esmeralda.
12 Cassatt, A. J., ch. f. **Abaca**, King Alfonso, Jamaica.*
13 Cassatt, A. J., b. f. ——, Stratford, Maudina.*
14 Davis & Hall, b. f. **Little Ella**, Little Phil, Ella Warfield.
15 Dwyer Bros., b. f. **Blue Dress**, Enquirer, Bribery.
16 Dwyer Bros., b. f. **Red Dress**, King Alfonso, Lilly Duke.
17 Dwyer Bros, b. f. ——, Enquirer, Colossa.
18 Empire Stable, b. f. **Gertie D.**, Dalnacardoch, Preciosa.
19 Empire Stable, b. f. **Miss Rhodie**, Milner, Rebecca.*
20 Gray & Co., b. f. **Edith Gray**, Ten Broeck, Alice Gray.
21 Gray & Co., b. f. **Tulla Blackburn**, Luke Blackburn, Tullahoma.
22 Hearst, Geo., b. f. **Gloaming**, Sir Modred, Twilight.
23 Hearst, Geo., b. f. **Golden Horn**, Spendthrift, Constantinople.
24 Hearst, Geo., blk. f. **Everglade**, Iroquois, Agenoria.
25 Hearst, Geo., ch. f. **Cosette**, Joe Hooker, Abbie W.
26 McCarty, D. J. & Bro., ch. f. **Pandora**, Rayon d'Or, Blue Grass Belle.
27 Madden, J. E., ch. f. **Grace Ely**, Onondaga, Fouwitch.*
28 Morris, G. B., b. f. **Tigress**, Billet, Vega.*
29 Morris, J. A. & A. H., ch. f. **Druidess**, Stonehenge, Castaguette.
30 Morris, J. A. & A. H., ch. f. **Homœopathy**, Reform, Maggie B. B.
31 Morris, J. A. & A. H., br. f. **Starlight**, Iroquois, Vandalite.
32 Morris, J. A. & A. H., b. f. **Frailty**, Prince Charlie, Blunder.*
33 Morris, J. A. & A. H., ch. f. **Mamie Russell**, Eolus, Tillie Russell.*
34 Murphy, James (Mrs. John M. Clay), b. f. **Kinesem**, Longfellow, Sylph.*
35 Nassau Stable, b. f. **Elize**, Reform, North Anna.
36 Nassau Stable, ch. f. **Pauline F.**, Hopeful, Buxom.
37 Preakness Stable, br. f. **Livonia**, Longfellow, Elkhorn Lass.
38 Preakness Stable, b. f. **Flossie**, Powhattan, Amethyst.
39 Scott, W. L., ch. f. **Minuet**, Rayon d'Or, Reel Dance.
40 Scott, W. L., ch. f. **Paradox**, Rayon d'Or, Lizzie Cox.
41 Scott, W. L., ch. f. **Martha**, Rayon d'Or, Lucy Wallace.
42 Shippee, L. U., ch. f. **Whisban**, King Ban, Whisperine.*
43 Stone, Kinzea (Mrs. John M. Clay), ch. f. **Equal Rights**, Himyar, Georgette.*
44 Withers, D. D., ch. f. **Bibelot**, King Ernest, Knicknack.
45 Withers, D. D., b. f. ——, King Ernest, Invermore.
46 Yale Stable, b. f. **Fannie C.**, Democrat, Moonlight.*
47 Yale Stable, ch. f. **Phoebe**, St. Blaise, Mehallah.

*Declared January 1st, 1890.

FIFTH RACE. — For three years old and upward. A sweepstakes of $15 each, with $750 added, of which $100 to second, and $50 to third. WEIGHTS AT 20 LBS. ABOVE THE SCALE. Non-winners in 1889 or 1890 of $2,000 allowed 7 lbs.; of $1,500, 10 lbs.; of $1,000, 15 lbs.; of $600, if three years old, 20 lbs.; if four years old and upward, 30 lbs.　**Seven Furlongs.**

SIXTH RACE. — For all ages. A sweepstakes of $15 each, with $750 added, of which $100 to second, and $50 to third. The winner to be sold at auction for $2,000; if entered to be sold for less 1 lb., allowed for each $100 down to $1,000; then 2 lbs. for each $100 down to $500.　**Six Furlongs.**

SIXTH DAY. — FRIDAY, JUNE 6TH.

FIRST RACE. — For three years old and upward that have run and not won in 1890 a race of $1,000. A sweepstakes of $15 each, with $750 added, of which $100 to second, and $50 to third. Non-winners in 1890 of $600, or of two races of any value, allowed 10 lbs. Maidens allowed 15 lbs.
One Mile and a Sixteenth.

SECOND RACE. — EL ARROYO HANDICAP, for all ages. A sweepstakes of $25 each, or $5 if declared, with $1,250 added, of which $250 to second, and $100 to third. Entries to be made on Wednesday, June 4th. Weights to be announced and declarations to be made on Thursday, June 5th.
One Mile and a Furlong.

THIRD RACE. — For maidens two years old. A sweepstakes of $15 each, with $750 added, of which $100 to second, and $50 to third. Those that have started and not run second in a race of the value of $2,000, allowed 5 lbs. **Five Furlongs.**

FOURTH RACE. — For three years old. A sweepstakes of $15 each, with $750 added, of which $100 to second, and $50 to third. The winner to be sold at auction for $5,000; if entered to be sold for $4,000, allowed 5 lbs.; if for $2,500, allowed 12 lbs.
One Mile and a Furlong.

FIFTH RACE. — For two years old. A sweepstakes of $15 each, with $750 added, of which $100 to second, and $50 to third. The winner to be sold at auction for $5,000; if entered to be sold for $4,000, allowed 5 lbs.; if for $3,000, 12 lbs.; if for $2,000, 20 lbs. **Five Furlongs.**

SIXTH RACE. — For three years old and upward. A sweepstakes of $15 each, with $750 added, of which $100 to second, and $50 to third. The winner to be sold at auction for $5,000; if entered to be sold for $4,000, allowed 5 lbs.; if for $3,000, 10 lbs.; then 1 lb. allowed for each $100 down to $1,500. **One Mile.**

FIRST RACE.—For three years old that have never won $1,000. A sweepstakes of $20 each, with $1,000 added, of which $200 to second, and $100 to third. Beaten maidens allowed 7 lbs.
One Mile and a Furlong.

SECOND RACE.—ERDENHEIM WELTER HANDICAP, for three years old and upward. A sweepstakes of $20 each, or $5 if declared, with $1,000 added, of which $200 to second, and $100 to third. Entries to be made on Thursday, June 5th. Weights to be announced and declarations to be made on Friday, June 6th.
Six Furlongs.

THIRD RACE.—BOWLING BROOK HANDICAP, for three years old. A sweepstakes of $100 each, h.f., or only $20 if declared, with $2,000 added, of which $500 to second, and $200 to third. Weights to be published February 1st, and declarations to be made February 20th. Closed January 2d, 1890, with 85 entries.
One Mile and a Furlong.

```
 1 Morris, J. A. & A. H., ch. c. Cayuga, Iroquois, Letola . . . . . . . .123
 2 Scott, W. L., ch. c. Torso, Algerine, Santa Lucia* . . . . . . . . . .122
 3 Belmont, August, ch. c. Padishah, St. Blaise, Sultana* . . . . . . .120
 4 Palo Alto S. F., b. c. Racine, Bishop, Fairy Rose* . . . . . . . . . .119
 5 Dwyer Bros., b. c. Blackburn, Luke Blackburn, Tomboy* . . . .119
 6 Scott, W. L., ch. g. Chaos, Rayon d'Or, Lilly R. . . . . . . . . . . .119
 7 Dwyer Bros., b. c. June Day, Falsetto, Virga* . . . . . . . . . . . .118
 8 Hough Bros., b. c. Drizzle, Ventilator, Mag . . . . . . . . . . . . .118
 9 Madison Stable, b. c. Devotee, Alarm, Sister of Mercy . . . . . . .118
10 Warnke, H. & Son, blk. f. Reclare, Reform, Clara . . . . . . . . . .118
11 Corrigan, Ed., b. c. Riley, Longfellow, Geneva . . . . . . . . . . .116
12 Pulsifer, D. T., blk. c. Onaway, Onondaga, Kelp . . . . . . . . . .116
13 Palo Alto S. F., ch. c. Flambeau, Wildidle, Flirt* . . . . . . . . . .116
14 Hearst, Geo., br. c. Tournament, Sir Modred, Plaything . . . . .115
15 New York Stable, b. c. Successor, Vauxhall, Sequence . . . . . . .115
16 Campbell, R. E., br. c. Protection, Prince Charlie, Manola . . . . .115
17 Hearst, Geo., b. c. Ballarat, Sir Modred, La Favorita . . . . . . .115
18 Scott, W. L., b. g. Banquet, Rayon d'Or, Ella T. . . . . . . . . . .114
19 Withers, D. D., b. c. ——, Kinglike, Fanfan . . . . . . . . . . . .114
20 Hearst, Geo., br. f. Miss Belle, Prince Charlie, Linnet . . . . . . .113
21 Dwyer Bros., b. c. Sir John, Sir Modred, Marian . . . . . . . . . .113
22 Empire Stable, ch. c. Tormentor, Joe Hooker, Callie Smart . . . .113
23 Dwyer Bros., ch. c. Caldwell, Ten Broeck, Miss Nailer . . . . . .112
24 Pulsifer, D. T., blk. c. Ralph Bayard, Muscovy, Imperatrice* . . .112
25 Scott, W. L., ch. c. Leighton, Rayon d'Or, L'Argentine . . . . . .112
26 Withers, D. D., b. c. ——, King Ernest, Cyclone . . . . . . . . . .110
27 Walbaum, G., ch. c. Rancocas, Iroquois, Ontario . . . . . . . . . .110
28 Morris, J. A. & A. H., br. f. Starlight, Iroquois, Vandalite . . . .110
29 Kraemer, A., br. c. Gramercy, Emperor, Felicity . . . . . . . . . .109
30 Santa Anita Stable, b. c. Santiago, Grinstead, Clara D. . . . : . . .108
31 Morris, J. A. & A. H., ch. f. Druidess, Stonehenge, Castagnette . . .108
```

Seventh Day. — Saturday, June 7th.

32 Withers, D. D., b. c. ———, Stonehenge, Eccola **108**
33 Morris, G. B., b. c., **Lisimony**, Lisbon, Patrimony **108**
34 Hart, L., b. f. **Maggie K.**, Billet, Miss Annie **107**
35 Daly, W. C., ch. f. **Urbanna**, King Bolt, Sunmaid **107**
36 Davis & Hall, b. f. **Little Ella**, Little Phil, Ella Warfield **106**
37 Dwyer Bros., b. c. **Flatbush**, Glenelg, Florida **106**
38 Hearst, Geo., b. c. **Anaconda**, Spendthrift, Maid of Athol **106**
39 Scott, W. L., ch. f. **Paradox**, Rayon d'Or, Lizzie Cox* **106**
40 Belmont, August, b. f. **Amazon**, The Ill Used, Fair Barbarian **106**
41 Davis & Hall, ch. g. **Bavarian**, Longfield, Bavaria **105**
42 Keystone Stable, b. c. **Mr. Pelham**, St. Blaise, Dauntless **105**
43 Labold Bros., br. c. **Experience**, Prince Charlie, Myralla **105**
44 Hearst, Geo., ch. c. **Baggage**, Warwick, Maria F. **105**
45 Pulsifer, D. T., ch. g. **Punster Jr.**, Punster, Maud P. **105**
46 Dwyer Bros., b. c. **Houston**, Hindoo, Bourbon Belle **105**
47 Rice, Wm., ch. c. **Rafter**, Kantaka, Belle of Maywood **105**
48 Morris, J. A. & A. H., ch. f. **Homœopathy**, Reform, Maggie B. B. . . **105**
49 Scott, W. L., ch. g. **Maximus**, Reform, Rachel* **105**
50 Hearst, Geo., b. f., **Golden Horn**, Spendthrift, Constantinople . . . **104**
51 Empire Stable, b. c. **Favorite**, Fiddlesticks, Favonia **104**
52 Withers, D. D., b. c. **Chieftain**, Uncas, Chamois **103**
53 Preakness Stable, b. f. **Flossie**, Powhattan, Amethyst **103**
54 Hearst, Geo., b. c. **King Thomas**, King Ban, Maud Hampton **100**
55 Hearst, Geo., b. f. **Gloaming**, Sir Modred, Twilight **100**
56 Greener, J. G., ch. c. **Sam Doxey**, Casino, Sallie Norvell **100**
57 Belmont, August, b. c. **Clarendon**, St. Blaise, Clara **100**
58 Belmont, August, b. f. **Leda**, Kingfisher, Leightonia **100**
59 Brown, S. S., b. c. ———, Leonatus, Martina **100**
60 Barbee, Geo., ch. c. **Village King**, Frederick the Great, Pride of the
Village **100**
61 Hearst, Geo., b. c. **Sir Lancelot**, Sir Modred, Faustina **100**
62 Dwyer Bros., b. c. **Longford**, Longfellow, Semper Idem **100**
63 Santa Anita Stable, b. f. **Magdalena**, Glenelg, Malta **100**
64 Santa Anita Stable, b. c. **Clio**, Grinstead, Glenita **100**
65 Jennings, Wm., b. g. **Mohican**, Iroquois, Bertha **100**
66 Sunol Stable, b. c. **Varius**, Virgil, Chinook **100**
67 Cotton & Boyle, ch. c. **Masterlode**, Sir Modred or Kyrle Daly, Bessie
Peyton **100**
68 Shippee, L. U., b. c. **Fellowcharm**, Longfellow, Trinket **100**
69 Morris, J. A. & A. H., br. c. **Dr. Helmuth**, Sir Modred, Sweetbriar . **100**
70 Haggin, J. B., b. c. **Hawkstone**, Hindoo, Queen Maud **95**
71 Haggin, J. B., blk. c. **Fernwood**, Falsetto, Quickstep **95**
72 Maltese Villa S. F., b. c. **Abdiel**, Jocko, Cousin Peggy **95**
73 Beverwyck Stable, ch. f. **Can Can**, Prince Charlie, La Esmeralda . **95**
74 Morris, J. A. & A. H., ch. c. **King's Own**, Hopeful, Queen's Own . . **95**
75 Santa Anita Stable, ch. c. **Amigo**, Prince Charlie, Mission Belle . . . **95**
76 Preakness Stable, b. c. **Dundee**, Macduff, Virginia Bush **95**
77 Brown, S. S., gr. f. ———, Springbok, Jennie V. **95**
78 Brown, S. S., b. c. ———, Powhattan, Lady Jane **95**
79 Labold Bros., ch. c. **Isaac Lewis**, Prince Charlie, Bellona **90**
80 Scott, W. L., ch. c. **Franco**, Rayon d'Or, Florio* **90**
81 Haggin, J. B., ch. f. **Rosette**, Joe Hooker, Rosa B. **90**
82 Dwyer Bros., b. c. **Bluebird**, Billet, Mundane **90**
83 Walker, Wm., b. c. **Jim Wasson**, Ten Broeck, Fanny Ellis **90**
84 Walker, Wm., b. c. **B. B. Million**, Ten Broeck, Maggie H. **90**
85 Walker, Wm., ch. c. **Foxmede**, Falsetto, Britomarte **90**

* Declared Feb. 20, 1890.

FOURTH RACE. — ALL BREEZE STAKES, for all ages.

A sweepstakes of $50 each, $15 forfeit, with $1,250 added, of which $250 to second, and $100 to third. Winners in 1890 of $3,000 to carry 5 lbs. extra. Those never having won $5,000, allowed 7 lbs.; $2,500, 10 lbs.; $1,000, 14 lbs. Closed January 2d, 1890, with 73 entries. **Seven Furlongs.**

1 Auburndale Stable, ch. c. **King Hazem**, 3, King Ban, Hazem.
2 Belmont, August, b. f. **Fides**, 4, The Ill Used, Fillette.
3 Belmont, August, ch. g. **Chesapeake**, 3, St. Blaise, Sultana.
4 Beverwyck Stable, br. f. **Brown Princess**, 4, Prince Charlie, Nannie Black.
5 Beverwyck Stable, b. c. **Cassius**, 4, Longfellow, Southern Belle.
6 Bonchurch Stable, ch. c. **Ill Spent**, 3, Spendthrift, Ilia.
7 Bowie, Oden, ch. m. **Belle d'Or**, 5, Rayon d'Or, Belle Meade.
8 Bowie, Oden, ch. h. **Salvini**, 5, Sensation, Stella.
9 Brown, S. S., br. c. **Reporter**, 4, Enquirer, Bonnie Meade.
10 Brown, S. S., br. c. **Buddhist**, 4, Hindoo, Emma Hanly.
11 Brown, S. S., ch. c. **Cortez**, 4, King Alfonso, Invercauld.
12 Brown, S. S., ch. h. **Defaulter**, 5, Spendthrift, Authoress.
13 Burch, W. P., br. h. **Prather**, 5, Virgil, Lady Olive.
14 Davis & Hall, b. g. **Patrocles**, a, Kingfisher, Patience.
15 Davis & Hall, b. m. **Bess**, a, Fadladeen, Betsy.
16 Davis & Hall, b. f. **Little Ella**, 3, Little Phil, Ella Warfield.
17 Dwyer Bros., br. h. **Kingston**, 6, Spendthrift, Authoress.
18 Dwyer Bros., b. c. **Blackburn**, 3, Luke Blackburn, Tomboy.
19 Dwyer Bros., br. f. **Aurania**, 4, Virgil, Ann Fief.
20 Dwyer Bros., b. c. **Sir John**, 3, Sir Modred, Marian.
21 Empire Stable, br. c. **Madstone**, 4, Vanderbilt, Nina Turner.
22 Empire Stable, ch. c. **Tormentor**, 3, Joe Hooker, Callie Smart.
23 Empire Stable, b. g. **Trestle**, 3, Kyrle Daly, Trellis.
24 Gebhard, F., b. g. **Volunteer II.**, 6, Mortemer, Sly Boots.
25 Gideon, D., b. c. **French Park**, 4, King Ban, Lou Pike.
26 Gideon, D., b. g. **Stonington**, 4, Hurrah or Pizarro, Quandary.
27 Gray & Co., bl. f. **Zoolite**, 4, Faustus, Zula.
28 Haggin, J. B., br. c. **Fitz James**, 5, Kyrle Daly, Electra.
29 Haggin, J. B. blk. c. **Fresno**, 4, Falsetto, Cachuca.
30 Haggin, J. B., blk. c. **Fernwood**, 3, Falsetto, Quickstep.
31 Haggin, J. B., b. c. **Hawkstone**, 3, Hindoo, Queen Maud.
32 Hearst, Geo., blk. m. **Gorgo**, 5, Isonomy, Flirt.
33 Hearst, Geo., b. c. **Ballarat**, 3, Sir Modred, La Favorita.
34 Hearst, Geo., br. f. **Miss Belle**, 3, Prince Charlie, Linnet.
35 Hearst, Geo., b. f. **Gloaming**, 3, Sir Modred, Twilight.
36 Hearst, Geo., b. f. **Golden Horn**, 3, Spendthrift, Constantinople.
37 Hearst, Geo., b. c. **Sir Lancelot**, 3, Sir Modred, Faustina.
38 Hearst, Geo., ch. c. **imp Del Mar**, 4, Somnus, Maid of the Hills.
39 Hearst, Geo., ch. f. **imp Gertrude**, 4, Somnus, Geraldine.
40 Hearst, Geo., ch. f. **Cosette**, 3, Joe Hooker, Abbie W.
41 Hodges & Austin, b. g. **Noonday**, 6, Kyrle Daly, Dawn.
42 Honig, D. A., br. g. **Cartoon**, 4, Reform, Clara.
43 Hough Bros., b. g. **Forest King**, 4, The Ill Used, Woodbine.
44 Israel, E. L., br. f. **Ocypete**, 3, Duke of Montrose, Olivia.
45 Labold Bros., b. m. **Leontine**, 5, Leonatus, Bonnie May.
46 Labold Bros., b. h. **Flitter**, 5, The Ill Used, Flibbertigibbet.
47 Lloyd, L., ch. g. **St. John**, a, Botheration, dam by Victory.
48 McCann, D. W., br. c. **Loantaka**, 4, Sensation, Peggy Dawdle.
49 McCoy, C. D., ch. c. **Beck**, 4, Bertram, Addie Hart.
50 McKane, R., ch. c. **Cracksman**, 4, Woodlands Sue Ryder.
51 Morris, G. B., b. c. **Lisimony**, 3, Lisbon, Patrimony.
52 Morris, J. A. & A. H., blk. h. **Britannic**, 6, Plevna, Faithless.
53 Morris, J. A. & A. H., ch. f. **Holiday**, 4, Hopeful, Minnie Mc.
54 Morris, J. A. & A. H., br. c. **Dr. Helmuth**, 3, Sir Modred, Sweetbriar.
55 Morris, J. A. & A. H., ch. f. **Druidess**, 3, Stonehenge, Castagnette.
56 Morris, J. A. & A. H., ch. f. **Homœopathy**, 3, Reform, Maggie B. B.

57 Mullins, J., b. h **Badge,** 5, The Ill Used, The Baroness.
58 Pincus, J., ch. f **Flora Ban,** 3, King Ban, Flora
59 Porter, F. P., ch. m. **Kate Bensberg,** 5, Respond, Mary II.
60 Pulsifer, D. T., ch. f. **Coots,** 4, Prince Charlie, Blunder.
61 Pulsifer, D. T., ch. g. **Punster Jr.,** 3, Punster, Maud P.
62 Pulsifer, D. T., b. c. **Tenny,** 4, Rayon d'Or, Belle of Maywood.
63 Rose, L. J., b. f. **Glenloch,** 3, Flood, Glenden.
64 Santa Anita Stable, ch. m. **Los Angeles,** 5, Glenelg, La Polka.
65 Santa Anita Stable, b. f. **Magdalena,** 3, Glenelg, Malta.
66 Santa Anita Stable, ch. c. **Sinaloa II.,** 3, Grinstead, Maggie Emerson.
67 Sattler, Chas., ch. c. **Gregory,** 3, Macaroon, Abundance.
68 Walbaum, G., ch. c. **Oregon,** 4, Onondaga, Skylight.
69 Walbaum, G., b. c. **Blue Rock,** 4, Billet, Calomel.
70 Walker, Wm., ch. c. **Syracuse,** 4, Saracen, Bijou.
71 Walker, Wm., ch. c. **Frontenac,** 3, Falsetto, Lerna.
72 Warnke, H. & Son, blk. f. **Reclare,** 3, Reform, Clara.
73 Western Union Stable, b. c. **Persuader,** 4, Dickens, Persuasion.

FIFTH RACE. — For two years old. A sweepstakes of $15 each, with $750 added, of which $100 to second, and $50 to third. The winner to be sold at auction for $2,500; if entered to be sold for less, 2 lbs. allowed for each $250 down to $2,000; then 3 lbs. for each $250 down to $1,500; then 2 lbs. for each $125 down to $1,000; then 3 lbs. for each $125 down to $500.

Five Furlongs.

SIXTH RACE. — For three years old and upward. A sweepstakes of $15 each, with $750 added, of which $100 to second, and $50 to third. The winner to be sold at auction for $3,000; if entered to be sold for $2,000, allowed 5 lbs.; if for less, 1 lb. for each $100 down to $1,000; then 2 lbs. for each $100 down to $500.

One Mile and a Sixteenth.

EIGHTH DAY.—TUESDAY, JUNE 10TH.

FIRST RACE. — For maiden fillies two years old. A sweepstakes of $15 each, with $750 added, of which $100 to second, and $50 to third. Those beaten and not having run second in a race of $2,000 allowed 5 lbs. **Five Furlongs.**

SECOND RACE. — PREAKNESS HANDICAP, for three years old and upward. A sweepstakes of $30 each, or $5 if declared, with $1,500 added, of which $300 to second, and $150 to third. Entries to be made on Saturday, June 7th. Weights to be announced and declarations to be made on Monday, June 9th.
One Mile and a Half.

THIRD RACE. — LARCHMONT STAKES, for two years old. A sweepstakes of $50 each, h.f., or only $10 if declared by April 1st, with $1,500 added, of which $300 to second, and $200 to third. Winner of a race of the value of $2,000, to carry 5 lbs. extra; or of two such races, or one of $5,000, 7 lbs. extra. Beaten maidens allowed 5 lbs. Closed January 2d, 1890, with 110 entries. **Six Furlongs.**

1 Aby, C. W., ch. c. **Rodman**, Rutherford, Leveret.
2 Auburndale Stable, br. c. **St. Crescent**, St. Blaise, Lorelle.
3 Belmont, August, b. c. **Masher**, The Ill Used, Magnetism.
4 Belmont, August, ch. f. **La Tosca**, St Blaise, Toucques.
5 Belmont, August, ch. g. **St. Patrick**, St. Blaise, Patience.
6 Belmont, August, ch. f. **Flavia**, St. Blaise, Flavina.
7 Belmont, August, ch. c. **St. Charles**, St. Blaise, Carita.
8 Belmont, August, ch. f. **Beauty**, St. Blaise, Bella.
9 Belmont, August, b. c. **Lipanto**, Kingfisher, Leightonia.
10 Belmont, August, ch. c. **Jack of Diamonds**, St. Blaise, Nellie James.
11 Beverwyck Stable, b. f. **Bertha Campbell**, King Alfonso, Vulpine.
12 Beverwyck Stable, b. c. **Craft**, Fellowcraft, Lady Himyar.
13 Brown, S. S., ch. c. ——, Richmond, Gladys.
14 Brown, S. S., ch. c. ——, Richmond, Mayfield.
15 Bruce, L. C., ch. c. **Brentano**, Great Tom, Addie Hart.
16 Conner, Wm. M., ch. c. **Glenbriar**, Glenelg, Susie Linwood.
17 Cotton, J., ch. c. ——, Pontiac, Lizzie Mack.
18 Daly, Marcus, ch. c. **Gold Dollar**, Sir Modred, Trade Dollar.
19 Daly, Marcus, ch. f. **Leonora**, Sir Modred, Lizzie Lucas.
20 Daly, Marcus, b. f. **Mistletoe**, Sir Modred, Letola.
21 Daly, Marcus, b. c. **Montana**, Ban Fox, Queen.
22 Daly, Marcus, b. f. **Namouna**, Sir Modred, La Favorita.
23 Daly, Marcus, b. c. **Prince Charming**, Sir Modred, Carissima.
24 Daly, Maurice, ch. c. **Silver King**, St. Blaise, Maud Hampton.
25 Davis & Hall, br. c. **Grafton**, Gaberlunzie, Olive Branch.
26 Doswell, Thos. W., ch. c. **Wilroy**, Wilful, Ecliptic.
27 Dwyer Bros., b. c. **Blacklock**, Billet, Jaconet.
28 Dwyer Bros., b. c. **Hempstead**, Hindoo, Emma Hanly.
29 Dwyer Bros., b. c., **Hannibal**, Hindoo, Mercedes.
30 Dwyer Bros., b. c. **Baychester**, Luke Blackburn, Silvermaid.
31 Dwyer Bros., b. c. **Great Guns**, Great Tom, Mariposa.
32 Dwyer Bros., br. c. **Bush Bolt**, Himyar, Booty.
33 Dwyer Bros., b. c. **Himlex**, Himyar, War Reel.

(40)

34 Dwyer Bros., blk. f. ——, Hindoo, Katie.
35 Empire Stable, b. c. **Lyceum**, Prince of Norfolk, Sister to Jim Douglass.
36 Empire Stable, ch. f. **Landscape**, Woodlands, Artifice.
37 Eureka Stable, b. c. **Happy George**, John Happy, Florine.
38 Evans, John, b. c. ——, Stratford, Relay.
39 Gray & Co., ch. c. **Quarterstretch**, Faustus, Tinsel.
40 Greener, Jno. G., b. c. **The Wandering Jew**, Kosciusko, Tecalote.
41 Hanover Stable, ch. c. ——, Powhattan, Sequence.
42 Hanson, W. B., br. c. **W. B. H.**, Enquirer, Babee.
43 Hearst, Geo., blk. f. **Firework**, Falsetto, Explosion.
44 Hearst, Geo., ch. c. **Algernon**, Joe Daniels, Faustina.
45 Hearst, Geo., ch. c. **Atlas**, Hyder Ali, Fidelity.
46 Hearst, Geo., b. c. **Warpath**, Ban Fox or Warwick, Second Hand.
47 Hearst, Geo., ch. c. **Anarchist**, Joe Hooker, Chestnut Bell.
48 Hearst, Geo., ch. c. **Snow Ball**, Joe Hooker, Laura Winston.
49 Hearst, Geo., b. c. **J. B.**, Warwick, Maria F.
50 Hearst, Geo., b. c. **Yosemite**, Hyder Ali, Nellie Collier.
51 Hough Bros., br. c. ——, Stratford, Evelyn Carter.
52 Hough Bros., b. c. ——, Dutch Roller, Grenadine.
53 Hunter, John, ch. c. **Calcium**, Great Tom, Bonnie Belle.
54 Hunter, John, ch. c. **Orawampum**, Onondaga, Nellie Booker.
55 Hunter, John, ch. g. **Tantrum**, Great Tom, Moselle.
56 Hunter, John, b. c. **Dictum**, Iroquois, Bonnie Meade.
57 Jennings, Wm., ch. c. **Kilrue**, Sir Modred, Tyranny.
58 Labold Bros., br. c. **Monterey**, Duke of Montrose, Patti.
59 Lakeland, Wm., br. c. **Willie L.**, Falsetto, Miranda.
60 Leach, Geo. T. blk. c. ——, Vocalic, Frances L.
61 Levi, Henry R., br. c. **Baltimore**, Stratford, Gazelle.
62 McClelland, Byron, br. f. ——, Billet, Retreat.
63 McElmeel, E., ch. c. ——, Bend'Or, Eusebia.
64 Morris, G. B., b. g. **Strathmeath**, Strathmore, Flower of Meath.
65 Morris, J. A. & A. H., b. c. **Key West**, Glenelg, Florida.
66 Morris, J. A. & A. H., ch. c. **Dr. Hasbrouck**, Sir Modred, Sweetbriar.
67 Morris, J. A. & A. H., b. c. **Blithe**, Onondaga, Bliss.
68 Morris, J. A. & A. H., b. c. **Mileties**, Darebin, Mileta.
69 Morris, J. A. & A. H., b. c. **Russell**, Eolus, Tillie Russell.
70 Morris, J. A. & A. H., b. c. **Woodcutter**, Forester, Glendalia.
71 Morris, J. A. & A. H., br. f. **Ambulance**, Onondaga, Black Maria.
72 Morris, J. A. & A. H., b. f. **Vacation**, Tom Ochiltree, Minnie Mc.
73 Morris, J. A. & A. H., ch. f. **Reckon**, Pizarro, Perhaps.
74 Morris, J. A. & A. H., b. f. **Persistence**, Sir Modred, Parthenia.
75 Palo Alto S. F., ch. c. **Rinfax**, Argyle, Amelia.
76 Palo Alto S. F. ch. f. **Tearless**, Wildidle, Teardrop.
77 Palo Alto S. F., ch. f. **Rosebud**, Wildidle, Rosetta.
78 Preakness Stable, br. g. **Dunbarton**, Macduff, Virginia Bush.
79 Pulsifer, D. T., ch. c. **Sir George**, Spendthrift, Piccadilly.
80 Pulsifer, D. T., ch. c. **Judge Mitchell**, Stratford, Heatherbelle.
81 Pulsifer, D. T., b. c. **Kirkover**, Atilla, The Squaw.
82 Ramapo Stable, b. c. **John Lackland**, Runnymede, Soubrette.
83 Rancocas Stable, b. c. **Uncertainty**, Emperor, Quandary.
84 Rancocas Stable, b. c. **Sirocco**, Emperor, Breeze.
85 Rancocas Stable, b. f. **Vanity**, Rotherhill or Glenelg, Pride.
86 Rancocas Stable, ch. f. **Lima**, Pizarro, Gladiola.
87 Rancocas Stable, b. f. **Arrogance**. Emperor, Disdain.
88 Rollins, W. C., b. f. ——, Hock Hocking, Maid of the Mist.
89 Rose, L. J., b. c. **Conrad**. Flood, Goula.
90 Santa Anita Stable, b. c. **Ensenada**, Rutherford, Aritta.
91 Santa Anita Stable, b. f. **Ogarita**, Longfellow, Mission Belle.
92 Santa Anita Stable, b. c. **San Joaquin**, Longfellow, Santa Anita Belle.
93 Santa Anita Stable, b. f. **Esperanza**, Grinstead, Hermosa.
94 Santa Anita Stable, b. f. **Cleopatra**, Grinstead, Maggie Emerson.
95 Santa Anita Stable, ch. c. **El Carman**, Gano, Grey Anne.
96 Scott, W. L., b. c. —— Sensation, Aella.
97 Scott, W. L., ch. f. **Turmoil**, Rayon d'Or, Lilly R.
98 Scott, W. L., b. f. **Maywood**, Rayon d'Or, Belle of Maywood.

99 Scott, W. L. br. f. **Amulet**, Rayon d'Or, Presto.
100 Scott, W. L., ch. f. **Miss Ransom**, Rayon d'Or, Nellie Ransom.
101 Scott, W. L., ch. f. **Cutalong**, Rayon d'Or, Claudia.
102 Scott, W. L., ch. f. **Millrace**, Wanderer, Santa Lucia.
103 Street, S. W., b. c. **Uncle Al**, Mr. Pickwick, Maratana.
104 Stuart, Louis & Co., b. c. ——, Mr. Pickwick, Maggie Hunt.
105 Stuart, Louis & Co., b. c. ——, Long Taw or Mr. Pickwick, Vibrate.
106 Sunol Stable, ch. g. **Ptolemy**, Kyrle Daly, Echota.
107 Walbaum, G., br. f. **Claudina**, Iroquois, Boulotte.
108 Walden, Jeter, br. c. **Glenlochy**, Glenelg, Cameo.
109 Walker, Wm., b. c. **Silver Prince**, Spendthrift, Phoebe Mayflower.
110 Walker, Wm., b. c. **Sidney**, Spendthrift, Constantinople.

To be run under the auspices of the American Jockey Club.

FOURTH RACE. — BELMONT STAKES, for three years old. A sweepstakes of $100 each, h.f., or $20 if declared by July 1st, 1889, with $3,000 added, of which $500 to second, and $200 to third. Winners in 1890 of $2,000 to carry 3 lbs.; of two such races, or one of $3,500, 7 lbs.; of two races of $3,500, 10 lbs. extra. Non-winners of a sweepstakes for three years old allowed 5 lbs. Maidens allowed 10 lbs. Closed August 15th, 1888, with 136 entries. **One Mile and a Quarter.**

Old Scale of Weight.

1 Appleby & Johnson, ch. c. ——, Falsetto, Queen Victoria.
2 Appleby & Johnson, b. c. ——, King Alfonso, Traviata.*
3 Auburndale Stable, ch. c. **King Hazem**, King Ban, Hazem.
4 Bathgate, Chas. W., b. c. ——, Spendthrift, Janet.
5 Bathgate, Chas. W., ch. g. ——, Luke Blackburn, Longitude.
6 Belmont, August, b. c. **Clarendon**, St. Blaise, Clara.
7 Belmont, August, ch. c. **Padishah**, St. Blaise, Sultana.
8 Belmont, August, ch. c. **Chesapeake**, St. Blaise, Susquehanna.
9 Belmont, August, ch. c. **St. Carlo**, St. Blaise, Carina.
10 Belmont, August, ch. c. **St. James**, St. Blaise, Nellie James.†
11 Belmont, August, ch. c. **Belisarius**, St. Blaise, Bella.
12 Belmont, August, b. c. **Lord Dalmeny**, The Ill Used, Lady Rosebery.
13 Belmont, August, b. c. **Magnate**, The Ill Used, Magnetism.
14 Bowie, Oden, b. c. **Lordlike**, Vassal, Ladylike.
15 Bowie, Oden, ch. c. **Tennessean**, Vassal, Tennessee.
16 Brown, Ed. (Melbourne Stable), b. c. **Prodigal Son**, Pat Malloy, Homeward Bound.
17 Brown, S. S., b. c. ——, Geo. Kinney, Matinee.
18 Bryant, Sam'l (Melbourne Stable), b. c. **Flambeau**, Forester, Bounce.
19 Byrnes, M. (Melbourne Stable), br. c. **Fernwood**, Falsetto, Quickstep.
20 Byrnes, M., b. c. **Hawkstone**, Hindoo, Queen Maud.
21 Campbell, Robt., b. c. **King Charlie**, Prince Charlie, Manola.
22 Castle Stable, b. g. **Felix**, Kingfisher, Felicia.*
23 Castle Stable, ch. c. **Elkton**, Eolus, Helen.
24 Castle Stable, ch. g. ——, Milner, Maggie C.*
25 Castle Stable, b. c. ——, King Ernest, Cadence.*
26 Castle Stable, b. c. **Elmstone**, Stonehenge, Majority.
27 Conner, Wm. M., blk. c. **Dalsyrian**, Dalnacardoch, Syria.
28 Conner, Wm. M., ch. f. **Tampette**, Dalnacardoch, Waltz.
29 Conner, Wm. M., b. f. **Chimere**, Iroquois, Chimera.
30 Cotton & Boyle, b. c. ——, Joe Hooker, Kitten.
31 Dahlman, I. H. (W. L. Scott), ch. c. **Nashota**, Rayon d'Or, Liatunah.
32 Davis & Hall, ch. c. **Bavarian**, Longfield, Bavaria.
33 Dwyer Bros., ch. c. **Tip Top**, Great Tom, Mozelle.*
34 Dwyer Bros., b. c. **Last Chance**, Virgil, Regan.*
35 Dwyer Bros., blk. or br. c. ——, Virgil, Finework.
36 Dwyer Bros., b. or br. c. **Houston**, Hindoo, Bourbon Belle.

37 Dwyer Bros., b. c. **Bluebird**, Hindoo, Mundane.
38 Dwyer Bros., b. or br. c. **Courtlandt**, Hindoo, Katie.*
39 Dwyer Bros., ch. c. **Frisco**, Hindoo, Francesca.*
40 Dwyer Bros., ch. c. ——, Onondaga, Beatrice.*
41 Dwyer Bros., ch. c. **Last King**, King Ban, Puzzle.
42 Dwyer Bros., b. c. **Sir John**, Sir Modred, Marian.
43 Gideon, D. (John D. Morrissey), ch. c. **Vassar**, Tom Ochiltree, Jenny Mc-
   Kinney.
44 Gratz, W. (Melbourne Stable), b. c. **Middlesex**, Billet, Bettie Lewis.
45 Hearst, Geo., b. c. **Sir Lancelot**, Sir Modred, Faustina.
46 Hearst, Geo., b. c. **Ballarat**, Sir Modred, La Favorita.
47 Hearst, Geo., b. c. **King Thomas**, King Ban, Maud Hampton.
48 Hearst, Geo., b. c. ——, Kyrle Daly, My Love.
49 Hearst, Geo., b. c. **Tournament**, Sir Modred, Plaything.
50 Hearst, Geo., br. c. **Kingmaker**, Warwick, Sister to Jim Douglass.
51 Hearst, Geo., ch. c. **Mistral**, Hock Hocking, Maid of the Mist.†
52 Hearst, Geo., ch. c. **Baggage**, Kyrle Daly, Maria F.
53 Hearst, Geo., b. c. **Anaconda**, Spendthrift, Maid of Athol.
54 Hearst, Geo., b. f. **Golden Horn**, Spendthrift, Constantinople.
55 Hearst, Geo., b. f. **Gloaming**, Sir Modred, Twilight.
56 Hearst, Geo., blk. f. **Everglade**, Iroquois, Agenoria.
57 Hearst, Geo., b. f. ——, Warwick, Mileta.
58 Hearst, Geo., ch. f. **Barn Dance**, Warwick, Cinderella.
59 Henry, John (Melbourne Stable), b. c. **Binscarth**, Billet, Lucille Western.*
60 Henry, John (Melbourne Stable), ch. c. **Strathclair**, Onondaga, Lady
   Stockwell.
61 Hough Bros. (B. Riley), blk. c. **Burlington**, Powhattan, Invercauld.
62 Jennings, W. B. (W. P. Burch) (G. B. Morris), b. c. **Glenscot**, Glenelg,
   Queen of Scots.*
63 Jennings, W. B., ch. c. ——, Onondaga, Ballet.
64 Jennings, Wm., b. c. **Wyndham**, Warwick, Lorilla.
65 Kraemer & Pryor, br. c. **Gramercy**, Emperor, Felicity.
66 Labold Bros. (Melbourne Stable), b. c. **Sunderland**, Onondaga,
   Imogene.*
67 Labold Bros. (Melbourne Stable), b. or br. c. **Chevron**, Duke of Magenta,
   Kaskaskia.*
68 Lakeland, Wm. (A. J. Cassatt) (Wm. Walker) (Melbourne Stable), b. c.
   Phoenix, Mr. Pickwick, Bonnie Wood.
69 Lewis & Long, b. or br. c. **Cadaverous**, Miser, Tipperary Girl.
70 Lorillard, L. L., ch. c. **Sleipeur**, Mortemer, Breeze.
71 McClelland, Byron, b. c. **Sam Morse**, Leonatus, Scramble.*
72 McDonald, J. E., ch. c. ——, Prince Charlie, La Favorita.
73 McMahon, Wm. (A. J. Cassatt) (Thos. W. Doswell), b. c. **Eurochlydon**,
   Eolus, Majestic.
74 McMahon, Wm. (W. L. Scott), ch. c. **Volo**, Rayon d'Or, Voila.
75 McStea, O. B. (Wm. Walker) (Melbourne Stable), ch. c. **Heatherton**,
   Hindoo, Sungleam.
76 Madison Stable, br. c. **Australand**, Reform, Australind.†
77 Madison Stable, b. f. **Laurentia**, Fiddlesticks or Kingfisher or St. Blaise,
   Laurette.†
78 Madison Stable, b. f. **Tocsin**, Alarm, Auricula.*
79 Madison Stable, b f. **Sonora**, Spendthrift, Sinaloa.*
80 Madison Stable, ch. f. **Ballad**, Greenland. Sonnet.*
81 Madison Stable, b. c. **Devotee**, Alarm, Sister of Mercy.
82 Madison Stable, ch. c. **Prosit**, Springbok, Venora.*
83 Madison Stable, b. c. **Australitz**, Greenland, Australina.†
84 Madison Stable, b. c. **Iago**, Bend'Or, Billetdoux.
85 Maltese Villa Stock Farm, b. c. **Abdiel**, Jocko, Cousin Peggy.
86 Maltese Villa Stock Farm, b. c. **Achilles**, Norfolk, Thetis.*
87 Melbourne Stable, ch. c. **Palisade**, Powhattan, Indemnity.
88 Morris, G. B., b. c. **Lisimony**, Lisbon, Patrimony.
89 Morris, G. B., ch. c. **Jersey Pat**, Pat Malloy, Jersey Lass.
90 Morris, J. A. & A. H., ch. c. **Cayuga**, Iroquois, Letola.
91 Morris, J. A. & A. H., br. c. **Mucilage**, Kyrle Daly, Mura.
92 Morris, J. A. & A. H., ch. c. **King's Own**, Hopeful, Queen's Own.

93 Morris, J. A. & A. H., b. c. **Telephone**, Glenelg, Acoustic.
94 Morris. J. A. & A. H., ch. c. **Lady Killer**, King Alfonso, Flirtation.*
95 Morris, J. A. & A. H., br. c. **Dr. Helmuth**, Sir Modred, Sweetbriar.
96 Morris, J. A. & A. H., b. f. **Starlight**, Iroquois, Vandalite.
97 Morris, J. A. & A. H., b. f. **Despair**, Falsetto, Desolation.*
98 Morris, J. A. & A. H., b. f. **Chemistry**, Longfellow, Lenora.*
99 Morris, J. A. & A. H., b. c. ——, Hindoo, Jennie Blue.*
100 Murphy, Dennis (Madison Stable), b. or br. f. **Vera**, Greenland, Maggie J.†
101 Murphy, Dennis (Madison Stable), ch. c. **Ganador**, Greenland, Patti.†
102 Newton, H. A. (Melbourne Stable), b. or br. c. **Fakofan**, Falsetto, Patula.†
103 Pincus, J., gr. c. **Bluestone**, Falsetto, Geneva.
104 Pincus, J., ch. f ——, King Ban, Flora.
105 Preakness Stable, b. c. **Dundee**, Macduff, Virginia Bush.
106 Preakness Stable, b. c. **Windsor**, Warwick or Sir Modred, Lady Middleton.
107 Puryear, T. & Co., b. c. ——, Joe Hooker, Illusion.
108 Riley, B., b. c. **Barnegat**, Billet, Emma Hauly.
109 Santa Anita Stable, ch. c. **Amigo**, Prince Charlie, Mission Belle.
110 Santa Anita Stable, ch. c. **Guadaloupe**, Grinstead, Josie C.
111 Santa Anita Stable, br. c. **Costa Rica**, Grinstead, Althola.
112 Santa Anita Stable, b. c. **Santiago**, Grinstead, Clara D.
113 Santa Anita Stable, b. f. ——, Glenelg, Malta.
114 Santa Anita Stable, ch. c. **Honduras**, Grinstead, Jennie B.
115 Scott, W. L., ch. g. **Chaos**, Rayon d'Or, Lilly R.
116 Scott, W. L., ch. c. **Leighton**, Rayon d'Or, L'Argentine.
117 Scott, W. L., ch. c. **Franco**, Rayon d'Or, Florio.
118 Scott, W. L., b. g. **Banquet**, Rayon d'Or, Ella T.
119 Scott, W. L., ch. g. **Maximus**, Reform, Rachel.
120 Scott, W. L., ch. c. **Torso**, Algerine, Santa Lucia.
121 Scott, W. L., b. c. **Index**, Kantaka, Sheboygan.*
122 Scott, W. L., ch. c. **Canteen**, Kantaka, Maurine.
123 Scott, W. L., b. c. **Zor**, Kantaka, Lady Scarborough.
124 Scott, W. L., ch. f. **Paradox**, Rayon d'Or, Lizzie Cox.
125 Stuart, James, ch. c. ——, Stonehenge, Mary Buckley.‡
126 Taylor, Frank (W. L. Scott), ch. c. **Centaur**, Rayon d'Or, Luella.
127 Tucker, R., b. c. **Pullman**, Glengarry, Kathleen.*
128 Tucker, R., b. c. **Watterson**, Great Tom, Duchess.*
129 Walker, M. (Melbourne Stable), ch. c. **Coleraine**, Hindoo, Waif.
130 Walker, Wm. (Melbourne Stable), ch. c. **Foxmede**, Falsetto, Britomarte.
131 Walker, Wm. (Chas. Jordan) (Melbourne Stable), ch. c. **Frontenac**, Falsetto, Lerna.
132 Weir, P. T. (W. L. Scott), ch. c. **Rafter**, Kantaka, Belle of Maywood.
133 Williams, J. S. (W. L. Scott), ch. c. **Crawfish**, Rayon d'Or, Brenda.
134 Withers, D. D., b. c. ——, Uncas, Chamois.
135 Withers, D. D., br. c. ——, Uncas, Sweet Home.
136 Withers, D. D., b. c. ——, Kinglike, Fan Fan.

*Declared July 1st, 1889.   † Declared after July 1st, 1889.   ‡ Void.

FIFTH RACE. — For all ages. A sweepstakes of $15 each, with $750 added, of which $100 to second, and $50 to third. The winner to be sold at auction for $3,000; if entered to be sold for less, 1 lb. allowed for each $100 down to $500.

Five Furlongs.

SIXTH RACE. — For three years old and upward. A sweepstakes of $15 each, with $750 added, of which $100 to second, and $50 to third. The winner to be sold at auction for $5,000; if entered to be sold for $4,000, allowed 5 lbs.; if for $3,000, 10 lbs.; if for less, 1 lb. for each $100 down to $1,000.

One Mile and Three-Sixteenths.

NINTH DAY.—WEDNESDAY, JUNE 11TH.

FIRST RACE.—For two years old. A sweepstakes of $15 each, with $750 added, of which $100 to second, and $50 to third. Non-winners of $2,500 allowed 5 lbs.; of $1,000, 10 lbs. Beaten maidens allowed 15 lbs. **Six Furlongs.**

SECOND RACE.—RANCHO DEL PASO HANDICAP, for three years old and upward. A sweepstakes of $25 each, or $5 if declared, with $1,250 added, of which $250 to second, and $100 to third. Entries to be made on Monday, June 9th. Weights to be announced and declarations to be made on Tuesday, June 10th. **One Mile and a Sixteenth.**

THIRD RACE.—BAYCHESTER STAKES, for three years old which have not won a race of $1,000 in 1889. A sweepstakes of $50 each, $15 forfeit, with $1,250 added, of which $250 to second, and $100 to third. Beaten maidens allowed 5 lbs. Closed January 2d, 1890, with 87 entries. **One Mile.**

1 Auburndale Stable, ch. c. **King Hazem**, King Ban, Hazem.
2 Barbee, Geo., ch. c. **Village King**, Frederick the Great, Pride of the Village.
3 Belmont, August, b. c. **Clarendon**, St. Blaise, Clara.
4 Belmont, August, ch. g. **Chesapeake**, St. Blaise, Susquehanna.
5 Belmont, August, b. f. **Leda**, Kingfisher, Leightonia.
6 Beverwyck Stable, b. f. **Minuet**, Glenelg, La Polka.
7 Beverwyck Stable, ch. f. **Can Can**, Prince Charlie, La Esmeralda.
8 Bonchurch Stable, ch. c. **Ill Spent**, Spendthrift, Ilia.
9 Bowie, Oden, ch. c. **Tennessean**, Vassal, Tennessee.
10 Bowie, Oden, br. g. ——, Vassal, Catamaran.
11 Bowie, Oden, b. f. **Alarm Bell**, Alarm, Belle Meade.
12 Boyle & Littlefield, br. c. ——, Virgil, Fannie Brown.
13 Brown, S. S., b. c. ——, Leonatus, Martina.
14 Brown, S. S., b. c. ——, Powhattan, Lady Jane.
15 Brown, S. S., gr. f. ——, Springbok, Jennie V.
16 Castle Stable, ch. c. **Elkton**, Eolus, Helen.
17 Cotton & Boyle, ch. c. **Masterlode**, Sir Modred or Kyrle Daly, Bessie Peyton.
18 Cotton & Boyle, b. c. **Architect**, Norfolk or Joe Hooker, Kitten.
19 Davis & Hall, br. f. **Iowa**, Iroquois, Cyrilla.
20 Davis & Hall, b. c. **Fad**, Fadladeen, Betsy.
21 Dwyer Bros., b. c. **Longford**, Longfellow, Semper Idem.
22 Dwyer Bros., b. c. **Sir John**, Sir Modred, Marian.
23 Dwyer Bros., b. c. **Flatbush**, Glenelg, Florida.
24 Dwyer Bros., b. c. **Houston**, Hindoo, Bourbon Belle.
25 Dwyer Bros., b. c. **Bluebird**, Billet, Mundane.
26 Dwyer Bros., b. c. **Kingsbridge**, Spendthrift, Kapanga.
27 Empire Stable, ch. c. **Tormentor**, Joe Hooker, Callie Smart.
28 Empire Stable, b. g. **Trestle**, Kyrle Daly, Trellis.

29 Greener, Jno. G., ch. c. **Sam Doxey**, Casino, Sallie Norvell.
30 Haggin, J. B., blk. c. **Fernwood**, Falsetto, Quickstep.
31 Haggin, J. B., b. c. **Hawkstone**, Hindoo, Queen Maud.
32 Haggin, J. B., ch. f. **Rosette**, Joe Hooker, Rosa B.
33 Hearst, Geo., b. c. **Anaconda**, Spendthrift, Maid of Athol.
34 Hearst, Geo., b. c. **Sir Lancelot**, Sir Modred, Faustina.
35 Hearst, Geo., b. f. **Golden Horn**, Spendthrift, Constantinople.
36 Hearst, Geo., br. f. **Miss Belle**, Prince Charlie, Linnet.
37 Hearst, Geo., blk. f. **Everglade**, Iroquois, Agenoria.
38 Hearst, Geo., b. f. **Gloaming**, Sir Modred, Twilight.
39 Israel, E. L., b. f. **Ocypete**, Duke of Montrose, Olivia.
40 Jennings, W. B., ch. c. ——, Onondaga, Ballet.
41 Jennings, Wm., b. c. **Wyndham**, Warwick, Lorilla.
42 Keystone Stable, b. c. **Mr. Pelham**, St. Blaise, Dauntless.
43 Kraemer, A., br. c. **Gramercy**, Emperor, Felicity.
44 Labold Bros., ch. c. **Isaac Lewis**, Prince Charlie, Bellona.
45 McClelland, Bryon, b. c. **Lord Peyton**, Leonatus, Lady Peyton.
46 McCoy, C. D., ch. g. **Tom Finley**, Great Tom, Bonnie Lawn.
47 McKane, Robt., b. f. **Martha K.**, Capt. Flaherty, Sue Ryder.
48 McMahon & Co., ch. c. **Kempland**, Milner, Glorianne.
49 McMahon & Co., br. c. **Garrison**, Atilla, The Squaw.
50 McMahon & Co., br. g. **Sterling** (formerly Euroclydon), Eolus, Majestic.
51 McStea, O. B., ch. c. **Heatherton**, Hindoo, Sungleam.
52 Maltese Villa S. F., b. c. **Abdiel**, Jocko, Cousin Peggy.
53 Morris, G. B., b. c. **Lisimony**, Lisbon, Patrimony.
54 Morris, G. B., ch. c. **Jersey Pat**, Pat Malloy, Jersey Lass.
55 Morris, J. A. & A. H., br. c. **Dr. Helmuth**, Sir Modred, Sweetbriar.
56 Morris, J. A. & A. H., ch. c. **King's Own**, Hopeful, Queen's Own.
57 Morris, J. A. & A. H., b. c. **Telephone**, Glenelg, Acoustic.
58 Morris, J. A. & A. H., b. f. imp. **Haste**, Energy, Garonne.
59 New York Stable, b. c. **Successor**, Vauxhall, Sequence.
60 Ottman, Wm., b. f. ——, Reform, Issaquena.
61 Pincus, J., gr. g. **Granite**, Falsetto, Geneva.
62 Pincus, J., ch. f. **Flora Ban**, King Ban, Flora.
63 Preakness Stable, b. f. **Flossie**, Powhattan, Amethyst.
64 Preakness Stable, b. c. **Monroe**, Macduff, Bonnie Lizzie.
65 Preakness Stable, b. c. **Dundee**, Macduff, Virginia Bush.
66 Pulsifer, D. T., blk. c. **Ralph Bayard**, Muscovy, Imperatrice.
67 Pulsifer, D. T., ch. g. **Punster Jr.**, Punster, Maud P.
68 Ramapo Stable, br. f. **Windsor**, Runnymede, Girofle.
69 Rice, Wm., ch. c. **Rafter**, Kantaka, Belle of Maywood.
70 Riley, B., b. g. **Barnegat**, Billet, Emma Hanly.
71 Santa Anita Stable, b. c. **Clio**, Grinstead, Glenita.
72 Santa Anita Stable, ch. c. **Magdalena**, Glenelg, Malta.
73 Santa Anita Stable, ch. c. **Amigo**, Prince Charlie, Mission Belle.
74 Santa Anita Stable, b. f. **Atalanta**, Grinstead, Blossom.
75 Scott, W. L., ch. c. **Franco**, Rayon d'Or, Florio.
76 Scott, W. L., ch. f. **Minuet**, Rayon d'Or, Reel Dance.
77 Scott, W. L., ch. f. **Martha**, Rayon d'Or, Lucy Wallace.
78 Shippee, L. U., b. c. **Take Notice**, Prince Charlie, Nota Bene.
79 Todd, J., br. g. **Spend All**, Spendthrift, Fandango.
80 Walker, Wm., b. c. **B. B. Million**, Ten Broeck, Maggie H.
81 Walker, Wm., b. c. **Jim Wasson**, Ten Broeck, Fanny Ellis.
82 Walker, Wm., ch. c. **Foxmede**, Falsetto, Britomarte.
83 Withers, D. D., b. c. **Chieftain**, Uncas, Chamois.
84 Withers, D. D., b. c. **Adamant**, Stonehenge, Adage.
85 Withers, D. D., ch. c. ——, Kinglike, Maxim.
86 Withers, D. D. b. c. ——, Uncas, Sweethome.
87 Yale Stable, ch. f. **Phoebe**, St. Blaise, Mehallah.

FOURTH RACE. — FORT SCHUYLER STAKES, for all

ages. A sweepstakes of $50 each, $15 forfeit, with $1,250 added, of which $250 to second, and $100 to third. The winner to be sold at auction for $5,000. If entered by 4 P.M. on the day before the day appointed for the race to be sold for $3,000, allowed 8 lbs. ; then 1 lb. allowed for each $100 down to $2,000. Closed January 2d, 1890, with 53 entries.   **One Mile.**

1 Batchelor, J. A., b. c. **King William**, 3, King Alfonso, Traviata.
2 Belmont, August, b. f. **Belfuda**, 5, Kingfisher, Bellona.
3 Belmont, August, b. c. **Clarendon**, 3, St. Blaise, Clara.
4 Beverwyck Stable, b. c. **Cassius**, 4, Longfellow, Southern Belle.
5 Beverwyck Stable, b. m. **Clay Stockton**, 5, Longfellow, Lida Gaines,
6 Beverwyck Stable, b. c. **Castaway**, 4, Outcast, Lucy Lisle.
7 Blunt, Edmund, c. c. **Seymour**, 4, Stratford, Imelda.
8 Bowie, Oden, ch. h. **Salvini**, 5, Sensation, Stella.
9 Bowie, Oden, ch. g. **Vosburgh**, 5, Vassal, Australia.
10 Brown, S. S., b. c. **J. A. B.**, 4, Glenelg, M. A. B.
11 Brown, S. S., ch. c. **Cortez**, 4, King Alfonso, Invercauld.
12 Brown, S. S, ch. c. **Defaulter**, 5, Spendthrift, Authoress.
13 Burch, W. P., br. h. **Prather**, 5, Virgil, Lady Olive.
14 Castle Stable, blk. f. **Rainbow**, 3, Iroquois, Explosion.
15 Cotton & Boyle, gr. h. **Gray Dawn**, 5, Billet, Mary Clark.
16 Cotton & Boyle, b. f. **Duplicity**, 4, Reform, Artifice.
17 Daly, W. C., ch. g. **Bronzomarte**, 6, Rayon d'Or, Doncaster Lass.
18 Daly, W. C., b. c. **Civil Service**, 3, Reform, Bonnella.
19 Davis & Hall, b. g. **Patrocles**, a, Kingfisher, Patience.
20 Dwyer Bros., br. f. **Aurania**, 4, Virgil, Ann Fief.
21 Dwyer Bros., ch. c. **Caldwell**, 3, Ten Broeck. Miss Nailer.
22 Dwyer Bros., br. c. **Congress**, 3, Kyrle Daly, Eliza.
23 Forbes, Geo., br. c. **Brussels**, 4, Billet, Emily Fuller.
24 Forbes, Geo., br. c. **Lonely**, 4, Longfellow, Leveret.
25 Forbes, Geo , ch. c. **Guy Gray**, 4, Intruder, Alice Gray.
26 Gideon, D., b. c. **Taviston**, 4, Luke Blackburn, Silvermaid.
27 Haggin, J. B., br. c. **Fitz James**, 5, Kyrle Daly, Electra.
28 Haggin, J. B., blk. c. **Fernwood**, 3, Falsetto. Quickstep.
29 Haggin, J. B., b. c. **Hawkstone**, 3, Hindoo. Queen Maud.
30 Hanover Stable, ch. f. **Vivid**, 4, King Alfonso, Flash.
31 Honig, D. A., br. g. **Cartoon**, 4, Reform, Clara.
32 Labold Bros., b. h. **Flitter**, 5, The Ill Used, Flibbertigibbet.
33 Lakeland, Wm., ch. c. **Raymond G.**, 4, Eolus, Ninon.
34 Lakeland, Wm., ch. h. **Tattler**, a, Tom Ochiltree, Columbia.
35 McStea, O. B., ch. c. **Heatherton**, 3, Hindoo, Sungleam.
36 McStea, O. B., b. c. **Bravo**, 4, Bramble, Nevada.
37 McStea, O. B., br. h. **Now or Never**, 5, Stratford, Bye and Bye.
38 Morris, G. B., ch. c. **Tipstaff**, 4, Rayon d'Or or Kantaka, Verdict.
39 Morris, J. A. & A. H., b. c. **Mucilage**, 3, Kyrle Daly, Mura.
40 Morris, J. A. & A. H., b. c. **Telephone**, 3, Glenelg, Acoustic.
41 Pulsifer, D. T., blk. c. **Ralph Bayard**, 3, Muscovy, Imperatrice.
42 Pulsifer, D. T., b. c. **Donley**, 4, Longfellow, Pearl Tyler.
43 Pulsifer, D. T., ch. g. **Punster Jr.**, 3, Punster, Maud P.
44 Pulsifer, D. T., ch. f. **Coots**, 4, Prince Charlie, Blunder.
45 Rose, L. J., ch. g. **Mikado**, 6, Shiloh, Margery.
46 Santa Anita Stable, b. c. **Clio**, 3, Grinstead, Glenita.
47 Scott, W. L., ch. c. **Franco**, 3, Rayon d'Or, Florio.
48 Scott, W. L., ch. f. **Martha**, 3, Rayon d'Or, Lucy Wallace.
49 Scott, W. L., ch. f. **Minuet**, 3, Rayon d'Or, Reel Dance.
50 Street, S. W., ch. c. **Bellair**, 4, Rayon d'Or, Florence I.
51 Walker, Wm., ch. c. **Syracuse**, 4, Saracen, Bijou.
52 Western Union Stable, b. g. **Jim Clare**, a, Frank Harper or Planter, dam by Revolver.
53 Western Union Stable, b. c. **Persuader**, 4, Dickens, Persuasion.

FIFTH RACE. — For three years old and upward. A sweepstakes of $15 each, with $750 added, of which $100 to second, and $50 to third. Winners in 1890 of $5,000, or twice of $2,000, to carry 5 lbs. extra. Non-winners in 1890 of $1,000 allowed 7 lbs. If non-winners in 1889 or 1890, allowed 12 lbs. Maidens, if four years old and upward, allowed 20 lbs.
One Mile and Three-Sixteenths.

SIXTH RACE. — For three years old and upward. A sweepstakes of $15 each, with $750 added, of which $100 to second, and $50 to third. The winner to be sold at auction for $2,000. If entered to be sold for less, 1 lb. allowed for each $100 down to $1,500; then 2 lbs. for each $100 down to $1,000; then 3 lbs. for each $100 down to $500.
Seven Furlongs.

¾ Mile Straight

TENTH DAY.—THURSDAY, JUNE 12TH.

FIRST RACE.—For three years old and upward that have started in 1890 and not won. A sweepstakes of $15 each, with $750 added, of which $100 to second, and $50 to third. Non-winners at any time of $1,000 allowed 7 lbs. Maidens, if three years old, allowed 12 lbs.; if four and upward, 20 lbs.

One Mile and a Quarter.

SECOND RACE.—CHESTERBROOK HANDICAP, for three years old and upward. A sweepstakes of $30 each, or $5 if declared, with $1,500 added, of which $300 to second, and $150 to third. Entries to be made on Tuesday, June 10th. Weights to be announced and declarations to be made on Wednesday, June 11th.

One Mile and Three Furlongs.

THIRD RACE. — ANTICIPATION STAKES, for two years old. A sweepstakes of $100 each, h.f., or only $20 if declared by April 1st, with $2,000 added, of which $500 to second, and $200 to third. Winner of a race of the value of $2,500 to carry 5 lbs. extra; of two such races, 7 lbs.; of three such races, 10 lbs. Beaten maidens allowed 5 lbs. Closed January 2d, 1890, with 106 entries.

Six Furlongs.

1 Auburndale Stable, ch. c. ——, Ten Broeck, Belle of Nantura.
2 Aby, C. W., ch. c. **Rodman**, Rutherford, Leveret.
3 Belmont, August, b. c. **Masher**, The Ill Used, Magnetism.
4 Belmont, August, ch. f. **La Tosca**, St. Blaise, Toucquet.
5 Belmont, August, ch. g. **St. Patrick**, St. Blaise, Patience.
6 Belmont, August, ch. f. **Flavia**, St. Blaise, Flavina.
7 Belmont, August, ch. c. **St. Charles**, St. Blaise, Carita.
8 Belmont, August, ch. f. **Beauty**, St. Blaise, Bella.
9 Belmont, August, b. c. **Lepanto**, Kingfisher, Leightonia.
10 Belmont, August, ch. c. **Jack of Diamonds**, St. Blaise, Nellie James.
11 Belmont, August, blk. g. **Adair**, St. Blaise, Adosinda.
12 Beverwyck Stable, b. f. **Polly S.**, Pizarro, Amandine.
13 Beverwyck Stable, b. c. **Craft**, Fellowcraft, Lady Himyar.
14 Bonchurch Stable, b. c. **War Duke**, Duke of Montrose, Warover.
15 Brown, S. S., ch. c. ——, Richmond, Gladys.
16 Brown, S. S., ch. c. ——, Richmond, Mayfield.
17 Bruce, L. C., ch. c. **Brentano**, Great Tom, Addie Hart.
18 Castle Stable, b. c. **Thorndale**, Eolus, Lizzie Hazlewood.
19 Castle Stable, b. c. **Bermuda**, Bersan, Fair Lady.
20 Colaizza & Fisher, b. c. ——, Duke of Montrose, Lizzie S.
21 Conner, Wm. M., ch. c. **Glenbriar**, Glenelg, Susie Linwood.
22 Cotton, J., ch. c. ——, Pontiac, Lizzie Mack.
23 Daly, Marcus, ch. c. **Gold Dollar**, Sir Modred, Trade Dollar.
24 Daly, Marcus, ch. f. **Leonora**, Sir Modred, Lizzie Lucas.
25 Daly, Marcus, b. f. **Mistletoe**, Sir Modred, Letola.
26 Daly, Marcus, b. c. **Montana**, Ban Fox, Queen.

27 Daly, Marcus, b. f. **Namouna**, Sir Modred, La Favorita.
28 Daly, Marcus, b. c. **Prince Charming**, Sir Modred, Carissima.
29 Daly, Marcus, ch. c. **Silver King**, St. Blaise, Maud Hampton.
30 Davis & Hall, ch. c. **Keyser**, Luke Blackburn, Janet Norton.
31 Davis & Hall, br. c. **Grafton**, Gaberlunzie, Olive Branch.
32 Dwyer Bros., b. c. **Blacklock**, Billet, Jaconet.
33 Dwyer Bros., b. c. **Hempstead**, Hindoo, Emma Hanly.
34 Dwyer Bros., b. c. **Hannibal**, Hindoo, Mercedes.
35 Dwyer Bros., b. c. **Baychester**, Luke Blackburn, Silvermaid.
36 Dwyer Bros., b. c. **Great Guns**, Great Tom, Mariposa.
37 Dwyer Bros., br. c. **Bush Bolt**, Himyar, Booty.
38 Dwyer Bros., b. c. **Himlex**, Himyar, War Reel.
39 Dwyer Bros., blk. f. ——, Hindoo, Katie.
40 Empire Stable, b. c. **Lyceum**, Prince of Norfolk, Sister to Jim Douglass.
41 Empire Stable, ch. f. **Landscape**, Woodlands, Artifice.
42 Evans, John, b. c. ——, Stratford, Relay.
43 Gray & Co., ch. c. **Quarter Stretch**, Faustus, Tinsel.
44 Hanson, W. B., br. c. **W. B. H.**, Enquirer, Babee.
45 Hearst, Geo., blk. f. **Firework**, Falsetto, Explosion.
46 Hearst, Geo., ch. c. **Algernon**, Joe Daniels, Faustina.
47 Hearst, Geo., ch. c. **Atlas**, Hyder Ali, Fidelity.
48 Hearst, Geo., b. c. **Warpath**, Ban Fox or Warwick, Second Hand.
49 Hearst, Geo., b. c. **El Verano**, Hock Hocking, Vixen.
50 Hearst, Geo., b. c. **J. B.**, Warwick, Maria F.
51 Hearst, Geo., b. c. **Yosemite**, Hyder Ali, Nellie Collier.
52 Hough Bros., b. c. ——, Dutch Roller, Grenadine.
53 Hough Bros., b. f. **Queer Girl**, Himyar, Queen Ban.
54 Hunter, John, ch. c. **Hoodlum**, Joe Daniels, Miss Clay.
55 Hunter, John, b. c. **Dictum**, Iroquois, Bonnie Meade.
56 Hunter, John, b. c. **Kiawah**, Iroquois, Buttercup.
57 Hunter, John, ch. g. **Conundrum**, Enquirer, Tassel.
58 Labold Bros, br. c. **Monterey**, Duke of Montrose, Patti.
59 Levi, Henry R., b. c. **Annapolis**, Alarm, Blossom.
60 Levi, Henry R., br. c. **Baltimore**, Stratford, Gazelle.
61 McClelland, Byron, br. f. ——, Billet, Retreat.
62 McCoy, C. D., ch. g. **Postmaster**, Enquirer, Bonetta.
63 McElmeel, E., ch. c. ——, Bend'Or, Eusebia.
64 Morris, G. B., b. c. **Lawrence**, Longfellow, Miss Lawrence.
65 Morris, J. A. & A. H., b. c. **Key West**, Glenelg, Florida.
66 Morris, J. A. & A. H., ch. c. **Dr. Hasbrouck**, Sir Modred, Sweetbriar.
67 Morris, J. A. & A. H., b. c. **Mileties**, Darebin, Mileta.
68 Morris, J. A. & A. H., b. c. **Russell**, Eolus, Tillie Russell.
69 Morris, J. A. & A. H., b. c. **Woodcutter**, Forester, Glendalia.
70 Morris, J. A. & A. H., b. c. **Blithe**, Onondaga, Bliss.
71 Morris, J. A. & A. H., b. c. **Westchester**, Glenelg, Ann Fief.
72 Morris, J. A. & A. H., br. f. **Ambulance**, Onondaga, Black Maria.
73 Morris, J. A. & A. H., b. f. **Persistence**, Sir Modred, Parthenia.
74 Morris, J. A. & A. H., ch. f. **Reckon**, Pizarro, Perhaps.
75 Morris, J. A. & A. H., b. f. **Vacation**, Tom Ochiltree, Minnie Mc.
76 New York Stable, ch. f. **Mauve**, Fonso, Mabille.
77 New York Stable, ch. g. **Pluto**, Fonso, Persia.
78 Palo Alto S. F., ch. c. **Rinfax**, Argyle, Amelia.
79 Palo Alto S. F., ch. f. **Tearless**, Wildidle, Teardrop.
80 Palo Alto S. F., ch. f. **Rosebud**, Wildidle, Rosetta.
81 Pulsifer, D. T., ch. c. **Sir George**, Spendthrift, Piccadilly.
82 Pulsifer, D. T., ch. c. **Judge Mitchell**, Stratford, Heatherbelle.
83 Pulsifer, D. T., b. c. **Kirkover**, Atilla, The Squaw.
84 Rancocas Stable, b. c. **Uncertainty**, Emperor, Quandary.
85 Rancocas Stable, b. c. **Sirocco**, Emperor, Breeze.
86 Rancocas Stable, b. f. **Vanity,**, Rotherhill or Glenelg, Pride.
87 Rancocas Stable, b. f. **Heiress**, Rotherhill, Finance.
88 Rancocas Stable, b. f. **Arrogance**, Emperor, Disdain.
89 Rose, L. J., br. f. **Peri**, Flood, Frolic.
90 Santa Anita Stable, b. c. **Ensenada**, Rutherford, Aritta.
91 Santa Anita Stable, b. c. **San Joaquin**, Longfellow, Santa Anita Belle.

(50)

92 Santa Anita Stable, b. f. **Esperanza**, Grinstead, Hermosa.
93 Santa Anita Stable, b. f. **Cleopatra**, Grinstead, Maggie Emerson.
94 Santa Anita Stable, b. f. **Ogarita**, Longfellow, Mission Belle.
95 Santa Anita Stable, ch. c. **Silverado**, Rutherford, Josie C.
96 Santa Anita Stable, b. f. **Lacienga**, Grinstead, Jennie D.
97 Scott, W. L., ch. c. **Bolero**, Rayon d'Or, All Hands Around.
98 Scott, W. L., b. c. **Versatile**, Rayon d'Or, Valleria.
99 Scott, W. L., ch. f. **Miss Ransom**, Rayon d'Or, Nellie Ransom.
100 Scott, W. L., br. f. **Amulet**, Rayon d'Or, Presto.
101 Scott, W. L., b. f. **Fugitive**, Wanderer, Honey Bee.
102 Scott, W. L., b. c. ——, Sensation, Aella.
103 Sunol Stable, ch. c. **Rheingold**, Bend'Or, Woodlark.
104 Walden, Jeter, b. c. **Ely**, Elias Lawrence, Lady Kelley.
105 Walker, Wm., b. c. **Silver Prince**, Spendthrift, Phoebe Mayflower.
106 Walker, Wm., b. c. **Sydney**, Spendthrift, Constantinople.

FOURTH RACE. — TRIAL STAKES, for three years old.

A sweepstakes of $100 each, h.f., or only $20 if declared by April 1st, with $3,000 added, of which $500 to second, and $300 to third. Winners in 1890 of a race of $4,000, or of two of $2,000, to carry 5 lbs. extra. Closed January 2d, 1890, with 55 entries.

One Mile and a Quarter.

1 Auburndale Stable, ch. g. ——, Harry O'Fallon, Sue Finnie.
2 Barbee, Geo., ch. c. **Village King**, Frederick the Great, Pride of the Village.
3 Belmont, August, ch. c. **St. Carlo**, St. Blaise, Carina.
4 Belmont, August, b. c. **Clarendon**, St. Blaise, Clara.
5 Belmont, August, ch. c. **Padishah**, St. Blaise, Sultana.
6 Belmont, August, ch. g. **Chesapeake**, St. Blaise, Susquehanna.
7 Belmont, August, b. c. **Magnate**, The Ill Used, Magnetism.
8 Beverwyck Stable, ch. f. **Can Can**, Prince Charlie, La Esmeralda.
9 Brown, S. S., b. c. ——, Leonatus, Martina.
10 Brown, S. S., b. c. ——, Powhattan, Lady Jane.
11 Corrigan, Ed., b. c. **Riley**, Longfellow, Geneva.
12 Dwyer Bros., b. c. **Longford**, Longfellow, Semper Idem.
13 Dwyer Bros., b. c. **June Day**, Falsetto, Virga.
14 Dwyer Bros., ch. c. **Caldwell**, Ten Broeck, Miss Nailer.
15 Dwyer Bros., b. c. **Sir John**, Sir Modred, Marian.
16 Dwyer Bros., b. c. **Flatbush**, Glenelg, Florida.
17 Dwyer Bros., b. c. **Houston**, Hindoo, Bourbon Belle.
18 Dwyer Bros., b. c. **Blackburn**, Luke Blackburn, Tomboy.
19 Dwyer Bros., b. c. **Bluebird**, Billet, Mundane.
20 Empire Stable, ch. c. **Tormentor**, Joe Hooker, Callie Smart.
21 Hearst, Geo., b. c. **King Thomas**, King Ban, Maud Hampton.
22 Hearst, Geo., br. c. **Tournament**, Sir Modred, Plaything.
23 Hearst, Geo., b. c. **Anaconda**, Spendthrift, Maid of Athol.
24 Hearst, Geo., b. c. **Ballarat**, Sir Modred, La Favorita.
25 Hearst, Geo., ch. c. **Baggage**, Warwick, Maria F.
26 Hearst, Geo., b. c. **Sacramento**, Joe Hooker, Ada C.
27 Hough Bros., b. c. **Drizzle**, Ventilator, Mag.
28 Hough Bros., blk. c. **Burlington**, Powhattan, Invercauld.
29 Keystone Stable, b. c. **Mr. Pelham**, St. Blaise, Dauntless.
30 Kraemer, A., br. c. **Gramercy**, Emperor, Felicity.
31 Labold Bros., br. c. **Experience**, Prince Charlie, Myralia.
32 Madison Stable, b. c. **Iago**, Bend'Or, Billetdoux.
33 Morris, G. B., b. c. **Judge Morrow**, Vagabond, Moonlight.
34 Morris, J. A. & A. H., ch. c. **Cayuga**, Iroquois, Letola.
35 Morris, J. A. & A. H., ch. c. **King's Own**, Hopeful, Queen's Own.
36 Morris, J. A. & A. H., b. c. **Telephone**, Glenelg, Acoustic.
37 Morris, J. A. & A. H., br. f. **Starlight**, Iroquois, Vandalite.

38 Morris, J. A. & A. H., b. f. **Imp Haste**, Energy, Garonne.
39 New York Stable, b. c. **Successor**, Vauxhall, Sequence.
40 Palo Alto S. F., ch. c. **Flambeau**, Wildidle, Flirt.
41 Pincus, J., gr. g. **Granite**, Falsetto, Geneva.
42 Pulsifer, D. T., blk. c. **Onaway**, Onondaga, Kelp.
43 Riley, B., b. g. **Barnegat**, Billet, Emma Hanly.
44 Rose, L. J., b. g. **Rico**, Shannon, Fannie Lewis.
45 Santa Anita Stable, ch. f. **Sinaloa II.**, Grinstead, Maggie Emerson.
46 Santa Anita Stable, ch. c. **Honduras**, Grinstead, Jennie D.
47 Santa Anita Stable, ch. c. **Amigo**, Prince Charlie, Mission Belle.
48 Santa Anita Stable, b. c. **Clio**, Grinstead, Glenita.
49 Santa Anita Stable, b. c. **Santiago**, Grinstead, Clara D.
50 Scott, W. L., ch. g. **Chaos**, Rayon d'Or, Lilly R.
51 Scott, W. L., b. g. **Banquet**, Rayon d'Or, Ella T.
52 Scott, W. L., ch. c. **Franco**, Rayon d'Or, Florio.
53 Scott, W. L., ch. g. **Maximus**, Reform, Rachel.
54 Walbaum, G., b.'c. **Kenwood**, Falsetto, Katie Creel.
55 Warnke, H. & Son, blk. f. **Reclare**, Reform, Clara.

FIFTH RACE. — For two years old that have not won a race of $2,000. A sweepstakes of $20 each, with $1,000 added, of which $200 to second, and $100 to third. Beaten maidens allowed 5 lbs. **Five Furlongs.**

SIXTH RACE. — For three years old and upward. A sweepstakes of $15 each, with $750 added, of which $100 to second, and $50 to third. The winner to be sold for $2,500; if entered to be sold for less, 2 lbs. allowed for each $250 down to $2,000; then 3 lbs. for each $250 down to $1,500; then 2 lbs. for each $125 down to $1,000; then 3 lbs. for each $125 down to $500. **One Mile and a Furlong.**

ELEVENTH DAY.—FRIDAY, JUNE 13TH.

FIRST RACE. — For two years old that have run and not won at the meeting. A sweepstakes of $20 each, with $1,000 added, of which $200 to second, and $100 to third. Those beaten twice allowed 5 lbs.; thrice, 12 lbs. · **Six Furlongs.**

SECOND RACE. — For three years old that have run and not won at the meeting. A sweepstakes of $20 each, with $1,000 added, of which $200 to second, and $100 to third. Those beaten twice allowed 5 lbs.; thrice, 12 lbs. **One Mile and One-Sixteenth.**

THIRD RACE. — For three years old and upward that have run and not won at the meeting. A sweepstakes of $15 each, with $750 added, of which $100 to second, and $50 to third. Those beaten twice allowed 5 lbs.; thrice, 12 lbs.; four or more times, 20 lbs. **One Mile and Three-Sixteenths.**

FOURTH RACE. — For two years old. A sweepstakes of $15 each, with $750 added, of which $100 to second, and $50 to third. The winner to be sold at auction for $3,000; if entered to be sold for less, 2 lbs. allowed for each $250 down to $2,500; then 3 lbs. for each $250 down to $2,000; then 2 lbs. for each $125 down to $1,500; then 3 lbs. for each $125 down to $1,000. **Six Furlongs.**

FIFTH RACE. — For three years old. A sweepstakes of $15 each, with $750 added, of which $100 to second, and $50 to third. The winner to be sold at auction for $3,000; if entered to be sold for less, 1 lb. allowed for each $100 down to $500. **One Mile.**

SIXTH RACE. — For all ages. A sweepstakes of $15 each, with $750 added, of which $100 to second, and $50 to third. The winner to be sold at auction for $3,000; if entered to be sold for $2,000, allowed 5 lbs.; if for less, 1 lb. for each $100 down to $1,000; then 2 lbs. for each $100 down to $500. **Five Furlongs.**

(53)

TWELFTH DAY. — SATURDAY, JUNE 14TH.

FIRST RACE. — RAMAPO WELTER HANDICAP, for three years old and upward. A sweepstakes of $20 each, or $5 if declared, with $1,000 added, of which $200 to second, and $100 to third. Entries to be made on Thursday, June 12th. Weights to be announced and declarations to be made on Friday, June 13th.

Seven Furlongs.

SECOND RACE. — THROGG'S NECK STAKES, for three years old. A sweepstakes of $50 each, $15 forfeit, with $1,250 added, of which $250 to second, and $100 to third. The winner to be sold at auction for $5,000. If entered by 4 P.M. on the day before the day appointed for the race to be sold for $3,000, allowed 8 lbs.; then 1 lb. allowed for each $100 down to $2,000. Beaten horses not liable to be claimed. Closed January 2d, 1890, with 60 entries.

Seven Furlongs.

1 Batchelor, J. A., b. c. **King William,** King Alfonso, Traviata.
2 Belmont, August, b. c. **Clarendon,** St. Blaise, Clara.
3 Belmont, August, b. f. **Leda,** Kingfisher, Leightonia.
4 Belmont, August, b. f. **Amazon,** The Ill Used, Fair Barbarian.
5 Bowie, Oden, b. c. **Lordlike,** Vassal, Ladylike.
6 Bowie, Oden, br. g. ——, Vassal, Catamaran.
7 Boyle & Littlefield, br. c. ——, Virgil, Fanny Brown.
8 Brown, S. S., b. c. ——, Ten Broeck, Belle of Nantura.
9 Brown, S. S., b. c. ——, Leonatus, Martina.
10 Brown, S. S., b. c. ——, Powhattan, Lady Jane.
11 Brown, S. S., b. c. ——, Longfellow, Anne Boleyn.
12 Burch, W. P., b. f. **Cornelia,** The Ill Used, Cordelia.
13 Cotton & Boyle, b. c. **Architect,** Norfolk or Joe Hooker, Kitten.
14 Cotton & Boyle, b. f. **Christine,** Kyrle Daly, Comanche.
15 Daly, W. C., b. c. **Civil Service,** Reform, Bonnella.
16 Davis & Hall, b. c. **Fad,** Fadladeen, Betsy.
17 Davis & Hall, ch. g. **Bavarian,** Longfield, Bavaria.
18 Dwyer Bros., ch. c. **Caldwell,** Ten Broeck, Miss Nailer.
19 Dwyer Bros., b. c. **Blackburn,** Luke Blackburn, Tomboy.
20 Dwyer Bros., b. c. **Extra Dry,** Glenelg, Peru.
21 Dwyer Bros., br. c. **Congress,** Kyrle Daly, Eliza.
22 Dwyer Bros., b. c. **Kingsbridge,** Spendthrift, Kapanga.
23 Dwyer Bros., b. c. **Bluebird,** Billet, Mundane.
24 Empire Stable, b. g. **Trestle,** Kyrle Daly, Trellis.
25 Haggin, J. B., blk. c. **Fernwood,** Falsetto, Quickstep.
26 Haggin, J. B., b. c. **Hawkstone,** Hindoo, Queen Maud.
27 Haggin, J. B., ch. f. **Rosette,** Joe Hooker, Rosa B.
28 Hart, L., b. f. **Maggie K.,** Billet, Miss Annie.
29 Hart, L., ch. f. ——, Geo. Kinney or Pat Malloy, Clemmie G.
30 Israel, E. L., b. f. **Ocypete,** Duke of Montrose, Olivia.
31 Jennings, W. B., ch. c. ——, Onondaga, Ballet.

32 Jennings, Wm., b. g. **Glen Fallon**, Glenmore, Infanta.
33 Jennings, Wm., b. g. **Mohican**, Iroquois, Bertha.
34 Keystone Stable, b. c. **Mr. Pelham**, St. Blaise, Dauntless.
35 Keystone Stable, b. f. **Insight**, Duke of Magenta, Perception.
36 Kraemer, A., br. c. **Gramercy**, Emperor, Felicity.
37 McClelland, Byron, b. c. **Lord Peyton**, Leonatus, Lady Peyton.
38 McCoy, C. D., ch. g. **Tom Finley**, Grea' Tom, Bonnie Lawn.
39 McMahon & Co., ch. c. **Kempland**, Milner, Glorianne.
40 McMahon & Co., br. c. **Garrison**, Atilla, The Squaw.
41 McMahon & Co., br. g. **Sterling** (formerly Euroclydon), Eolus, Majestic.
42 McStea, O. B., ch. c. **Heatherton**, Hindoo, Sungleam.
43 Morris, G. B., blk. c. **Vitality**, Vandal Jr., Ida B.
44 Morris, J. A. & A. H., b. c. **Mucilage**, Kyrle Daly, Mura.
45 Morris, J. A. & A. H., b. c. **Telephone**, Glenelg, Acoustic.
46 Morris, J. A. & A. H., br. c. **Dr. Helmuth**, Sir Modred, Sweetbriar.
47 Pincus, J., gr. g. **Granite**, Falsetto, Geneva.
48 Pincus, J., ch. f. **Flora Ban**, King Ban, Flora.
49 Preakness Stable, b. c. **Monroe**, Macduff, Bonnie Lizzie.
50 Preakness Stable, b. f. **Ruby Royal**, Macduff, Vintage.
51 Pulsifer, D. T., blk. c. **Ralph Bayard**, Muscovy. Imperatrice.
52 Pulsifer, D. T., ch. g. **Punster Jr.**, Punster, Maud P.
53 Riley, B., b. g. **Barnegat**, Billet, Emma Hanly.
54 Rose, L. J., b. f. **Glenloch**, Flood, Glendew.
55 Santa Anita Stable, b. c. **Clio**, Grinstead, Glenita.
56 Scott, W. L., ch. c. **Franco**, Rayon d'Or, Florio.
57 Scott, W. L., ch. f. **Minuet**, Rayon d'Or, Reel Dance.
58 Scott, W. L., ch. f. **Martha**, Rayon d'Or. Lucy Wallace.
59 Scott, W. L., ch. g. **Maximus**, Reform, Rachel.
60 Todd, J., br. g. **Spend All**, Spendthrift, Fandango.

THIRD RACE. — GREAT ECLIPSE STAKES, for two

years old. A sweepstakes of $250 each, h.f., or only $10 if declared by January 1st, 1890, or $25 if declared by April 1st, 1890, or $50 if declared by May 1st, 1890, with $10,000 added, of which $2.000 to second, and $1,000 to third. Closed August 15th, 1889, with 223 entries. **Six Furlongs.**

1 Auburndale Stable, b. c. **St. Crescent**, St. Blaise, Lorelle.
2 Auburndale Stable, b. c. **Duke John**, Duke of Montrose, Reina Victoria.
3 Auburndale Stable, ch. c. ——, Ten Broeck, Belle of Nantura.
4 Auburndale Stable, blk. or br. c. ——, Pizarro, Tea Rose.
5 Auburndale Stable, b. c. ——, Tympanum, Creda.
6 Belmont, August, b. c. **Lepanto**, Kingfisher, Leightonia.*
7 Belmont, August, b. c. **Fritz**, St. Blaise, Fillette.
8 Belmont, August, ch. c. **St. Patrick**, St. Blaise, Patience.
9 Belmont, August, b. c. **Masher**, The Ill Used, Magnetism.
10 Belmont, August, ch. c. **Potomac**, St. Blaise, Susquehanna.
11 Belmont, August, ch. g. **St. Omer**, St. Blaise, Olitipa.*
12 Belmont, August, ch. c. **Jack of Diamonds**, St. Blaise, Nellie James.*
13 Belmont, August, ch. c. **St. Charles**, St. Blaise, Carita.
14 Belmont, August, ch. f. **Beauty**, St. Blaise, Bella.
15 Belmont, August, b. f. **Semiramis**, St. Blaise, Sultana.*
16 Belmont, August, ch. f. **Flavia**, St. Blaise, Flavina.
17 Beverwyck Stable (B. G. Thomas), b. c. **Craft**, Fellowcraft, Lady Himyar.
18 Blunt, Edmund, b. c. **Somerset**, Stratford, Imelda.
19 Brady, P. (W. H. Cheppu), blk. f. ——, Volturno, Virgie Shepherd.
20 Brown, Ed., b. c. **Oberlin**, Onondaga, Glenora.
21 Brown, Ed. (B. G. Thomas), b. c. **Ben's Pet**, Himyar, Themis.
22 Brown, S. S., ch. c. ——, Richmond, Mayfield.
23 Brown, S. S., ch. c. ——, Richmond, La Cigale.*
24 Brown, S. S., ch. c. ——. Richmond, Gladys.

25 Bruce, L. C., ch. c. **Brentano**, Great Tom, Addie Hart.
26 Bruce, L. C., b. f. **Krikina**, Muscovy, Krik.
27 Bruce, L. C., blk. f. **Vocaletta**, Vocalic, Vietta.
28 Bryant, Sam'l, ch. c. **Eldora**, Springbok, Astora.
29 Castle Stable, b. c. ——, Glenelg, La Polka.
30 Castle Stable, b. c. ——, Glenelg, Return.
31 Clay, James B.. b. c. **Chesterton**, Longfellow, Insignia.*
32 Clay, James B., blk. f. **Mon Droit**, Falsetto, Playingfields.*
33 Coghlin, J. J. (T. J. Megibben), b. c. **Claude Melnotte**, Audrain, Madamoiselle.
34 Conner, Wm. M., ch. c. **Glenbriar**, Glenelg, Susie Linwood.
35 Conner, Wm. M., ch. f. **Furlano**, Woodlands, Waltz.
36 Conner, Wm. M., ch. f. **Gardelia**, Woodlands, Glidelia.
37 Conner, Wm. M., b. f. **Imperieuse**, Pizarro, Imogene.
38 Conner, Wm. M., br. f. **Beata**, Strathmore, Beatrice.
39 Corrigan, Ed., b. c. ——, Falsetto, Mary Howard.*
40 Corrigan, Ed., blk. f. ——, Powhattan, Hattie Harris.
41 Daly, Marcus, ch. c. ——, Sir Modred, Trade Dollar.
42 Daly, Marcus, b. c. ——, Sir Modred, Carissima.
43 Daly, Marcus, br. c. ——, Darebin, Agenoria.*
44 Daly, Marcus, b. c. ——, Ban Fox, Queen.
45 Daly, Marcus, ch. c. ——, St. Blaise, Maud Hampton.
46 Daly, Marcus, b. c. ——, John Happy, Susan.*
47 Daly, W. C., ch. c., **Best Boy**, Ten Broeck, Highflight.
48 Davis & Hall, ch. c. ——, Luke Blackburn, Janet Norton.
49 Davidson, J. H., b. c. **Hullnut**, Fonso, Impromptu.
50 Dwyer Bros., ch. c. **Young George**, Geo. Kinney, Arizona.*
51 Dwyer Bros., b. c. **Blacklock**, Billet, Jaconet.
52 Dwyer Bros., b. c. **Beware**, Billet, Distraction.
53 Dwyer Bros. b. c. **Hempstead**, Hindoo, Emma Hanly.
54 Dwyer Bros., b. c. **Longshore**, Longfellow, Sea Shell.
55 Dwyer Bros., b. c. **Headlight**, Hindoo, Delight.
56 Dwyer Bros., b. or br. c. **Westchester**, Falsetto, Semper Vive.*
57 Dwyer Bros., b. c. **Hannibal**, Hindoo, Mercedes.
58 Dwyer Bros., b. c. **Baldwin**, Enquirer, Bribery.
59 Dwyer Bros., b. c. **Baychester**, Luke Blackburn, Silvermaid.
60 Dwyer Bros., b. or br. c. **Great Guns**, Great Tom, Mariposa.
61 Dwyer Bros., b. c. **Envoy**, Enquirer, Tomboy.
62 Dwyer Bros., b. or br. f. ——, Hindoo, Bourbon Belle.
63 Dwyer Bros., blk. or br. f. ——, Hindoo, Katie.
64 Dwyer Bros., ch. f. ——, Hindoo, Manahatta.*
65 Dwyer Bros. (N. T. Harris), b. c. ——, Geo. Kinney, Kate Clark.
66 Dwyer Bros. (N. T. Harris), b. c. ——, Geo. Kinney, Coupon.
67 Dwyer Bros. (N. T. Harris), b. c. ——, Geo. Kinney, Kinney.
68 Dwyer Bros. (B. G. Thomas), b. c. **Himlex**, Himyar, War Reel.
69 Dwyer Bros. (B. G. Thomas), br. c. **Bush Bolt**, Himyar, Booty.
70 Dwyer Bros. (B. G. Thomas), ch. c. **Ourfellow**, Fellowcraft, Lena Oliver.
71 Empire Stable, b. c. **Lyceum**, Prince of Norfolk, Sister to Jim Douglass.
72 Empire Stable, ch. f. **Landscape**, Woodlands, Artifice.
73 Frazer, Edward, b. c. **Sir Thomas**, Himyar, Floss.
74 Gibbons, J. E., b. c. **Ammunition**, Farandole, Bird Shot.
75 Gideon, David (W. H. Cheppu), ch. c. ——, Miser, Bonaventure.
76 Gideon, David (N. T. Harris), b. f. ——, Geo. Kinney, Mayonnaise.*
77 Gray & Co., b. c. **Zender**, Faustus, Bank Stock.
78 Gray & Co., ch. c. **Ketchum**, Faustus, Annie Richards.
79 Haggin, J. B. (N. T. Harris), ch. c. ——, Geo. Kinney, Bijou.
80 Hannigan, John & Co., b. f. **Borealis**, Billet, Mattie Amelia.
81 Hannigan, John & Co. (McClelland & Roche), ch. c. ——, Hindoo, Morgan Girl.*
82 Hanover Stable (N. T. Harris), ch. f. ——, Neptune, Alma.*
83 Hanover Stable (Spendthrift Stud), ch. c. ——, Spendthrift, Torchlight.
84 Harlan Bros., br. c. ——, Vanderbilt, Nina Turner.
85 Hearst, Geo., b. c. ——, Warwick or Ban Fox, Second Hand.
86 Hearst, Geo., ch. c. ——, Joe Daniels, Faustina.
87 Hearst, Geo., blk. f. ——, Falsetto, Explosion.

1¼ mile Stretch

88 Hearst, Geo., ch. c. ——, Hyder Ali, Fidelity.
89 Hearst, Geo., ch. f. ——, Hyder Ali, Graciosa.
90 Hearst, Geo., b. c. **J. B.**, Warwick, Maria F.
91 Hearst, Geo., b. c. **Yosemite**, Hyder Ali, Nellie Collier.
92 Hearst, Geo., ch. c. **Anarchist**, Joe Hooker, Chestnut Belle.
93 Hearst, Geo., ch. c. **Charley Brown**, Jim Brown, Viola.
94 Hearst, Geo., ch. c. **Snow-Ball**, Joe Hooker, Laura Winston.
95 Holloway, R. T., b. c. **Wildwood**, Forester, Azalia.*
96 Hunter, John, ch. c. **Orawampum**, Onondaga, Nellie Booker.
97 Hunter, John, ch. c. **Hoodlum**, Joe Daniels, Miss Clay.
98 Hunter, John, b. c. **Kiawah**, Iroquois, Buttercup.
99 Hunter, John, ch. c. **Calcium**, Great Tom, Bonnie Bell.
100 Hunter, John, ch. c. **Conundrum**, Enquirer, Tassel.
101 Ingleside Place, ch. c. **The Kaiser**, Pizarro, Blomida.
102 Ireland Bros., b. c. **Woodvale**, Deceiver, Lady Crafton.
103 Jennings, Wm., ch. c. ——, Sir Modred, Tyranny.
104 Johnston, P. P., ch. c. **B. G. T.**, Himyar, Vitality.
105 Kellar, Murray (N. T. Harris), b. f. ——, Geo. Kinney, Midsummer.
106 Kernaghan, G. H., br. f. **Dodo**, Falsetto, Brocade.
107 Kernaghan, G. H., b. f. ——, Lisbon, Bertha B.
108 Kernaghan, G. H., b. f. ——, Duke of Montrose, Helen Wallace.
109 Kraus, Geo. J., b. c. **Happy George**, John Happy, Florine.
110 Labold Bros., br. c. **Elknoe**, Longfellow, Locust Boom.
111 Lakeland, A., b. f. **Madge L.**, Warwick or Darebin, Altitude.
112 Lakeland, A. (W. H. Cheppu), b. c. ——, Leonatus, Periwinkle.
113 Leigh, Eugene (T. J. Megibben), b. c. **Pisara**, Pizarro, Sister Monica.
114 Letcher, W. R. (James B. Clay), blk. c. **Pompet**, Longfellow, Fuschia.
115 Littlefield, Chas. (W. H. Cheppu), ch. c. Miser, Peradventure.
116 Littlefield, Chas. (B. G. Thomas), ch. c. **My Craft**, Fellowcraft, Hegiaz.*
117 Littlefield, Chas. (B. G. Thomas), ch. c. **Simrock**, Fellowcraft, Almira.
118 McCarty, D. J. & Bro., blk. f. ——, Joe Daniels, Test.
119 McGuigan, A., ch. c. **Chimes**, Onondaga, Fonwitch.
120 McClelland, Byron, ch. c. ——, Blue Eyes, Etna.*
121 McClelland, Byron (McClelland & Roche), ch. f. ——, Hindoo, Red and Blue.
122 Madden, J. E. (McClelland & Roche), b. c. ——, The Ruke, Flora Mc-
    Donald.
123 Madison Stable, ch. f. **Scotia**, Forester, Mollie Hart.*
124 Madison Stable, b. c. **Riot**, Jack Cade, Atalanta.*
125 Madison Stable, b. f. **Crutches**, Tom Ochiltree, Mollie Carew.
126 Madison Stable, b. c. **Rocket**, Voltigeur, Birdie B.*
127 Madison Stable, br. c. **Arctic**, Greenland, Lucette.*
128 Madison Stable, b. c. **Baritone**, Greenland, Patti.*
129 Madison Stable, ch. f. **Bonita**, Dalnacardoch, Preciosa.
130 Madison Stable, b. f. **Penitent**, Pardee, Essayez II.*
131 Madison Stable, ch. c. **Austral**, Reform, Australind.
132 Madison Stable, b. c. **Heel Taps**, Glenelg, Peru.
133 Maltese Villa Stock Farm, br. c. **King Atta**, Alta, Cousin Peggy.
134 Maltese Villa Stock Farm, b. c. **Sir Rae**, Alta, Constellation.
135 Megibben, J. K. & Co. (T. J. Megibben), ch. c. **McKinley**, Springbok,
    Zulite.
136 Megibben, J. K. & Co. (T. J. Megibben), ch. c. **Tom Reed**, Audrain,
    War Lass.
137 Mehrbach, Isidor (W. H. Cheppu), b. c. ——, Volturno, Emily F.
138 Mehrbach, Isidor (W. H. Cheppu), b. f. ——, Gunnar, Annie S.
139 Morris, G. B., b. g. **Strathmeath**, Strathmore, Flower of Meath.
140 Morris, J. A. & A. H., b. c. **Westchester**, Glenelg, Ann Fief.
141 Morris, J. A. & A. H., b. c. **Key West**, Glenelg, Florida.
142 Morris, J. A. & A. H., b. c. **Woodcutter**, Forester, Glendalia.
143 Morris, J. A. & A. H., b. or br. c. **Blithe**, Onondaga, Bliss.
144 Morris, J. A. & A. H., b. c. **Two Lips**, Darebin, Kiss-me-quick.*
145 Morris, J. A. & A. H., b. c. **Mileties**, Darebin, Mileta.
146 Morris, J. A. & A. H., ch. c. **Dr. Hasbrouck**, Sir Modred, Sweetbriar.
147 Morris, J. A. & A. H., b. c. **Russell**, Eolus, Tillie Russell.
148 Morris, J. A. & A. H., b. c. **Hands Off**, Luke Blackburn, Touch-me-not.*
149 Morris, J. A. & A. H., b. c. **Footlight**, Luke Blackburn, Toplight.*

150 Morris, J. A. & A. H., b. c. **Chatham**, St. Blaise, Clara.*
151 Morris, J. A. & A. H., b. c. **Missive**, Billet, Francesca.*
152 Morris, J. A. & A. H., b. c. **Mountain Deer**, Iroquois, Martica.*
153 Morris, J. A. & A. H., b. c. **Terrifier**, Alarm, Bonnella.*
154 Morris, J. A. & A. H., b. f. **Vacation**, Tom Ochiltree, Minnie Mc.
155 Morris, J. A. & A. H., b. f. **Lita**, Tom Ochiltree, Letty.*
156 Morris, J. A. & A. H., b. f. **All Hope**, Tom Ochiltree, Aspiration.*
157 Morris, J. A. & A. H., br. f. **False**, Tom Ochiltree, Faithless.*
158 Morris, J. A. & A. H., ch. f. **Affection**, St. Blaise, Affinity.
159 Morris, J. A. & A. H., br. f. **Arbutus**, Sir Modred or Darebin, Miss Woodford.*
160 Morris, J. A. & A. H., ch. f. **Glucose**, Kyrle Daly, Mura.*
161 Morris, J. A. & A. H., b. f. **Persistence**, Sir Modred, Parthenia.
162 Morris, J. A. & A. H., b. f. **Fresco**, Glenelg, Finework.
163 Morris, J. A. & A. H., b. f. **Ambulance**, Onondaga, Black Maria
164 Morris, J. A. & A. H., ch. f. **Reckon**, Pizarro, Perhaps.
165 Morris, J. A. & A. H., b f. **Zulu**, Pizarro, Zoo-Zoo.*
166 Morris, J. A. & A. H., b. f. **Compassion**, Alarm, Sister of Mercy.
167 Morris, J. A. & A. H. (B. G. Thomas), b. c. **Asben**, Petrarch, Astolat.
168 Munro, James & Co., ch. c. **Katerfelto**, Great Tom, Mary Washington.
169 Neil, Jack, ch. c. ——, Fonso, Aetna.
170 Nudine Stable, b. c. **Homer**, Shannon, Sallie Gardner.
171 Nudine Stable, ch. f. **Glenlivet**, Flood, Glendew.
172 Penny, Hugh (W. H. Cheppu), blk. c. ——, Volturno, Black Libby.
173 Preakness Stable, b. g. **Putnam**, Powhattan, Amethyst.*
174 Preakness Stable, br. g. **Dunbarton**, Macduff, Virginia Bush.
175 Rancocas Stable, b. c. **Sirocco**, Emperor, Breeze.
176 Rancocas Stable, br. c. **Happy Day**, Emperor, Felicity.
177 Rancocas Stable, b. f. **Pandora**, Emperor, Susan Ann.*
178 Rancocas Stable, b. f. **Arrogance**, Emperor, Disdain.
179 Rancocas Stable, ch. f. **Portia**, Joe Daniels, Sly Dance.*
180 Rancocas Stable, br. f. **Morgheda**, Iroquois, Marchioness.*
181 Rancocas Stable, ch. f. **Lima**, Pizarro, Gladiola.
182 Rancocas Stable, b. or br. f. **Varina**, Pizarro, Virginia Wallace.*
183 Rancocas Stable (B. G. Thomas), ch. c. **Catlan**, Cymbal, The Cat.
184 Rand, C. E. (Spendthrift Stud), ch. c. ——, Spendthrift, Doubt.
185 Reed, Chas. & Sons, b. c. **Sextus**, Long Taw, Belle of the Meade.
186 Reed, Chas. & Sons, ch. c. **Trinity**, Forester, British Beauty.
187 Reed, Chas. & Sons, b. c. **Hallenbeck**, Mr. Pickwick, Sarong.
188 Reed, Chas. & Sons, ch. c. **Benjamin**, Mr. Pickwick, Countess.
189 Reedy, Frank J. (Spendthrift Stud), b. f. ——, Dutch Roller, Excellenza.
190 Sands, Wm. H., b. c. ——, Kyrle Daly, Trellis.
191 Scoggan Bros., b. f. **Lady Washington**, Miser, Minnarette.
192 Scoggan Bros., b. c. **Eli Kindig**, Geo. Kinney, Leona.
193 Scott, W. L., b. c. **Versatile**, Rayon d'Or, Valleria.
194 Scott, W. L., ch. c. **Bolero**, Rayon d'Or, All Hands Around.
195 Scott, W. L., b. c. **Pestilence**, Wanderer, Quarantine.
196 Scott, W. L., b. or br. f. **Amulet**, Rayon d'Or, Presto.
197 Scott, W. L., b. f. **Fugitive**, Wanderer, Honey Bee.
198 Scott, W. L., ch. f. **Seashore**, Wanderer, Lison.
199 Scott, W. L., b. f. **Maywood**, Rayon d'Or, Belle of Maywood.
200 Scott, W. L., ch. f. **Millrace**, Wanderer, Santa Lucia.
201 Scott, W. L., ch. f. **Miss Ransom**, Rayon d'Or, Nellie Ransom.
202 Shippee, L. U., b. c. **Lodowic**, Longfellow, Carrie Phillips.
203 Shippee, L. U., b. f. **False Queen**, Falsetto, Queen Victoria.
204 Shreve, T. W. (W. H. Cheppu), br. f. ——, Volturno, Merry Lass.
205 Spendthrift Stud, b. c. ——, Spendthrift, Janet.*
206 Spendthrift Stud, ch. f. ——, Spendthrift, Kapanga.
207 Spendthrift Stud, b. f. ——, Spendthrift, Miramir.
208 Spendthrift Stud, blk. c. ——, Onondaga, My Nannie O.
209 Spendthrift Stud, b. c. ——, Dutch Roller, Grenadine.
210 Spendthrift Stud (Chas. W. Bathgate), ch. c. ——, Spendthrift, Longitude.*
211 Stanley, F. G., b. c. **Bob Arthur**, Saxon, Pearl Tyler.*
212 Thompson, Andrew, b. or br. c. ——, Great Tom, Duchess.

213 Thompson, Andrew (A. Lakeland), ch. c. **Sheepshead**, Rotherhill, Pauline Sprague.
214 Thornton, H. I., br. c. **Austrian**, Darebin, Bavaria.
215 Thornton, H. I., br. f. **Bessie Barnes**, Darebin. Carrie C.
216 Thornton, H. I., ch. c. **Memnon**, Three Cheers, Aurora.*
217 Walbaum, G. (D. J. McCarty & Bro.), gr. c. ——, Blazes, Emma Hawison (Emma H.).
218 Walcott, A. F., b. c. ——, Mr. Pickwick, Maratana.
219 Walden, Jeter, br. f. **Katrina**, Sir Modred or Kyrle Daly, Miss Laura.
220 Walker, Wm. (Spendthrift Stud), b. c. ——, Spendthrift, Phoebe May-flower.
221 Walker, Wm. (Spendthrift Stud) b. c. ——, Spendthrift, Constantinople.
222 Williams, J. T., ch. c. ——, King Alfonso, Pearl Thorn.
223 Wood, W. G., b. c. **King Silver**, Silvermine, Miss Mickey.

*Declared Jan. 1, 1890.

FOURTH RACE. — WESTCHESTER CUP, for all ages.

A sweepstakes of $100 each, h.f., or only $20 if declared by April 1st, with $3,000 added, of which $500 to second, and $300 to third. Winner in 1890 of $5,000, when carrying weight for age or more, to carry 5 lbs. extra. Closed January 2d, 1890, with 34 entries.

One Mile and a Half.

1 Armstrong, S. P., b. h. **Juggler**, 5, Jils Johnson, Avoca.
2 Beverwyck Stable, b. m. **Lavinia Belle**, 5, Longfellow, Belle Knight.
3 Brown, S. S., br. f. **Senorita**, 4, Prince Charlie, Gondola.
4 Brown, S. S., br. c. **Reporter**, 4, Enquirer, Bonnie Meade.
5 Brown, S. S., br. c. **Buddhist**, 4, Hindoo, Emma Hanly.
6 Brown, S. S., ch. c. **Cortez**, 4, King Alfonso, Invercauld.
7 Castle Stable, b. c. **Diablo**, 4, Eolus, Grace Darling.
8 Corrigan, Ed., b. c. **Riley**, 3, Longfellow, Geneva.
9 Dwyer Bros., br. h. **Kingston**, 6, Spendthrift, Kapanga.
10 Dwyer Bros., b. c. **Blackburn**, 3, Luke Blackburn, Tomboy.
11 Dwyer Bros., b. c. **Longstreet**, 4, Longfellow, Semper Idem.
12 Dwyer Bros., b. h. **Sir Dixon**, 5, Billet, Jaconet.
13 Haggin, J. B., b. m. **Firenzi**, 6, Glenelg, Florida.
14 Haggin, J. B., ch. c. **Salvator**, 4, Prince Charlie, Salina.
15 Hearst, Geo., ch. c. **Baggage**, 3, Warwick, Maria F.
16 Hearst, Geo., ch. c. **Almont**, 4, Three Cheers, Question.
17 Hough Bros. b. g. **Come to Taw**, 4, Long Taw, Mollie Seabrook.
18 Keystone Stable, b. c. **Mr. Pelham**, 3, St. Blaise, Dauntless.
19 Labold Bros., br. h. **Montrose**, 6, Duke of Montrose, Patti.
20 Labold Bros., br. f. **Retrieve**, 4, Duke of Montrose, Patti.
21 Montana Stable, ch. c. **Spokane**, 4, Hyder Ali, Interpose.
22 Morris, G. B., b. c. **Eric**, 4, Duke of Magenta, Second Hand.
23 Morris, J. A. & A. H., ch. c. **Cayuga**, 3, Iroquois, Letola.
24 Mullins, J., b. h. **Badge**, 5, The Ill Used, The Baroness.
25 New York Stable, b. c. **Successor**, 3, Vauxhall, Sequence.
26 Pulsifer, D. T., b. c. **Tenny**, 4, Rayon d'Or, Belle of Maywood.
27 Pulsifer, D. T., blk. c. **Onaway**, 3, Onondaga, Kelp.
28 Rose, L. J., ch. c. **Rover**, 3, Wildidle, Rosetta.
29 Santa Anita Stable, ch. m. **Los Angeles**, 5, Glenelg, La Polka.
30 Santa Anita Stable, ch. c. **Honduras**, 3, Grinstead, Jennie B.
31 Santa Anita Stable, b. c. **Santiago**, 3, Grinstead, Clara D.
32 Stewart, Jno. T. & Son, ch. f. **Verdeur**, 4, Vandal Jr. or Democrat, Minnie K.
33 Walbaum, G., ch. c. **Sorrento**, 4, Joe Hooker, Rosa B.
34 Western Union Stable, b. h. **Dunboyne**, 6, Uncas, Frey.

FIFTH RACE. — For two years old. A sweepstakes of $15 each, with $750 added, of which $100 to second, and $50 to third. Horses entered not to be sold to carry full weight; those entered to be sold for $4,000, allowed 5 lbs.; if for $2,500, allowed 12 lbs.

Six Furlongs.

SIXTH RACE. — ANNIESWOOD HANDICAP, for three years old and upward. A sweepstakes of $20 each, or $5 if declared, with $1,000 added, of which $200 to second, and $100 to third. Entries to be made on Thursday, June 12th. Weights to be announced and declarations to be made on Friday, June 13th.

One Mile and a Quarter.

NOTICE.

———

ALL payments for Entrance Money, Forfeits, etc., must be made to W. L. POWERS, Clerk of the Course and Scales, or to his assistant, who will in all cases furnish a printed voucher. The club will not be responsible for any claim on account of payments made or alleged to have been made unless a receipt be produced in proof thereof.

———

ALL applications for Stabling must be addressed to the Executive Committee, through the Superintendent,

W. A. GORMAN,

MORRIS PARK,

West Chester, N. Y.

———

To Owners, Trainers, and Jockeys.

ALL Badges for the Meeting will be issued at the Park only by the Superintendent.

SCALE OF WEIGHT FOR AGE.

DISTANCE.	AGE.	OLD.		NEW.	
		May.	June.	May.	June.
Half Mile . . .	2 years .	80	82	84	86
	3 " .	106	107	110	111
	4 " .	118	118	122	122
	5, 6 & aged	121	120	125	124
Three-quarters of a Mile . .	2 years .	76	77	80	81
	3 " .	106	107	110	111
	4 " .	118	118	122	122
	5, 6 & aged	120	120	124	124
One Mile . . .	2 years .	75	75	79	79
	3 " .	102	103	106	107
	4 " .	118	118	122	122
	5, 6 & aged	122	122	126	126
One Mile and a Half	3 years .	100	101	104	105
	4 " .	118	118	122	122
	5 " .	123	122	127	126
	6 & aged .	124	123	128	127
Two Miles . .	3 years .	98	99	102	103
	4 " .	118	118	122	122
	5 " .	124	123	128	127
	6 & aged .	125	124	129	128
Two Miles and a Half	3 years .	97	98	101	102
	4 " .	118	118	122	122
	5 " .	125	124	129	128
	6 & aged .	126	125	130	129
Three Miles . .	3 years .	96	97	100	101
	4 " .	118	118	122	122
	5 " .	126	125	130	129
	6 & aged .	127	126	131	130
Four Miles . .	3 years .	95	96	99	100
	4 " .	118	118	122	122
	5 " .	127	126	131	130
	6 & aged .	128	127	132	131

In races of intermediate lengths, the weights for the shorter distance are to be carried.

In races exclusively for three-year-olds, or for four-year-olds, the weight shall be 122 lbs.: and in races exclusively for two-year-olds, the weight shall be 118 lbs.

Except in handicaps, and in races where the weights are fixed absolutely in the conditions, fillies two years old shall be allowed 3 lbs.; and mares three years old and upward, shall be allowed 5 lbs.

Under the Old Scale, in races exclusively for three-year-olds, the weight shall be 118 lbs., and for two-year-olds, 115 lbs.; and geldings, of all ages, are entitled to an allowance of 3 lbs.

CONDITIONS AND REGULATIONS
OF THIS MEETING.

On race days, entries will close thirty minutes after the last race; on other days, at 4 P.M.

When not otherwise stated in the conditions of the race, weights for handicaps will be announced after the last race on the day before the race, and declarations made through the entry-box thirty minutes thereafter.

Entry blanks will be furnished at the Course, and must be filled in full with description, name, age, pedigree, weight, colors, and allowances.

Owners and trainers must be careful to claim allowances, and are responsible for the weight carried.

Entries and probable starters will be announced immediately after the hour for closing.

If a horse be disqualified on account of incorrect weight, the decision shall not apply to bets, provided the weight published in the programme, or corrected on the notice board, was carried.

In all cases, horses must be struck out thirty minutes before the time appointed for the race to be run, and from that moment all horses remaining in shall be considered starters, as far as the betting is concerned.

If more than one horse, the property of the same owner, be entered for a selling purse, the entry shall not be void, but the horse first named shall alone be eligible to start.

An entry by telegram, received in time, will be accepted as though made through the entry-box.

Winner of a specified sum means winner of a single race of that value.

In all selling races, the half of any surplus on the sale of the winner shall go to the second horse, and the other half of any such surplus shall go to the fund for disabled jockeys.

Jockeys must weigh in twenty minutes before the time set for the race in which they are to ride.

The Club reserves the right to change or withdraw entirely any unclosed race.

Owners not having funds to their credit on the books of the Club, will be required to pay the Forfeit or Entrance Fee before their jockey can pass the scales.

Horses must be saddled in the paddock, unless excused by the Judges.

T. H. KOCK,   H. DE COURCY FORBES,
  Secretary.   *President.*

NEW YORK JOCKEY CLUB.

FALL MEETING, 1890.

October 1st to October 15th,

STAKES CLOSED.

RACE.	Age.	Distance.	Add. Money.	No. Entries.
White Plains Handicap	2	$3/4$ m.	$10,000	270
Dunmow Stakes . . .	2	$3/4$ m.	5,000	228
Fashion Stakes . . .	F.2	$3/4$ m.	1,250	138
Titan Stakes * . . .	2	1400 yds	5,000	135
Nursery Stakes * . . .	2	$3/4$ m.	2,000	123
Farewell Stakes . . .	2	$3/4$ m.	1,000	93
Jerome Stakes * . . .	3	$1^5/_{16}$ m.	2,500	127
Mosholu Stakes * . .	3	$1^1/_8$ m.	2,500	127
Protectory Stakes . .	3	1 m.	1,250	115
Hunter Stakes * . . .	F.3	$1^3/_{16}$ m.	2,000	97
Pelham Bay Handicap .	3	$1^5/_8$ m.	5,000	90
Hickory Stakes . . .	3	$1^1/_2$ m.	10,000	83
Peytona Stakes . . .	F.3	$1^1/_8$ m.	1,250	58
Echo Stakes.	3	$1^1/_{16}$ m.	1,000	57
Country Club Handicap	All.	$1^1/_8$ m.	2,000	98
New Rochelle Stakes	All.	$1^1/_4$ m.	2,500	82

* To be run under the auspices of the American Jockey Club.

Superintendent's Residence

STAKES

TO CLOSE AUGUST 15th, 1890.

———

Spring Meeting 1891

Fall Meeting 1891

Spring Meeting 1892

Fall Meeting 1892

NEW YORK JOCKEY CLUB.

Special attention is called to the following

STAKES

to close August 15th, 1890.

SPRING MEETING 1891.

JUVENILE STAKES, for Two Years Old. A sweepstakes of $100 each, h.f., or only $10 if declared by January 1st, 1891, or $20 if declared by April 1st, 1891, with **$2,000** added, of which $500 to second, and $200 to third. **HALF A MILE.**

GREAT ECLIPSE STAKES, for Two Years Old. A sweepstakes of $250 each, h.f., or only $10 if declared by January 1st, 1891, or $25 if declared by April 1st, 1891, or $50 if declared by May 1st, 1891, with **$10,000** added, of which $2,000 to second, and $1,000 to third. **SIX FURLONGS.**

FALL MEETING 1891.

NURSERY STAKES, for Two Years Old. A sweepstakes of $150 each, h.f., or only $10 if declared by January 1st, 1891, or $25 if declared by August 1st, 1891, with **$5,000** added, of which $1,000 to second, and $500 to third. Winners of two races of $5,000, or one of $10,000 to carry 5 lbs. extra; of two of $10,000, or one of $20,000, 10 lbs. extra. Non-winners of $1,000 allowed 5 lbs. Beaten maidens allowed 7 lbs. **SIX FURLONGS.**

SPRING MEETING 1892.

WITHERS STAKES, for Three Years Old.
A sweepstakes of $100 each, h.f., or only $10 if declared by January 1st, 1891, or $20 if declared by January 1st, 1892, or $30 if declared by April 1st, 1892, with **$3,000** added, of which $500 to second, and $200 to third.

ONE MILE.

BELMONT STAKES, for Three Years Old. A sweepstakes of $100 each, h.f., or only $10 if declared by January 1st, 1891, or $20 if declared by January 1st, 1892, or $30 if declared by April 1st, 1892, with **$3,000** added, of which $500 to second, and $300 to third. The winner of the Withers Stakes to carry 7 lbs. extra.

ONE MILE AND A QUARTER.

LADIES' STAKES, for Fillies Three Years Old. A sweepstakes of $100 each, h.f., or only $10 if declared by January 1st, 1891, or $20 if declared by January 1st, 1892, or $30 if declared by April 1st, 1892, with **$2,000** added, of which $500 to second, and $200 to third. **ONE MILE AND A FURLONG.**

FALL MEETING 1892.

HUNTER STAKES, for Fillies Three Years Old. A sweepstakes of $100 each, h.f., or only $10 if declared by January 1st, 1891, or $20 if declared by January 1st, 1892, or $30 if declared by August 1st, 1892, with **$2,000** added, of which $500 to second, and $200 to third. Winners in 1892 of two races of $3,000, or one of $5,000, to carry 5 lbs. extra; of two of $5,000, or one of $10,000, 7 lbs. extra. Non-winners at any time of $1,000 allowed 7 lbs. Beaten maidens 12 lbs.

ONE MILE AND A HALF.

JEROME STAKES, for Three Years Old. A sweepstakes of $250 each, h.f., or only $10 if declared by January 1st, 1891, or $25 if declared by January 1st, 1892, or $50 if declared by August 1st, 1892, with **$10,-000** added, of which $2,000 to second, and $1,000 to third. The winner of any race exclusively for three years old, of the value of $5,000, to carry 3 lbs. extra; of two such races, 5 lbs. extra; of three such races or one of $20,000, 7 lbs. extra. Beaten maidens allowed 5 lbs.

ONE MILE AND A HALF.

H. DE COURCY FORBES,   T. H. KOCK,
President.   *Secretary.*

Offices: 5th Avenue and 22d Street, New York.

FASTEST TIME ON RECORD.

Dash Races.

DISTANCE.		TIME.
¼.	JIM MILLER, 2, Deer Lodge (Mont.), Aug. 16th, 1888	0:21½
⅜.	CYCLONE (a), Helena (Montana), Aug. 29th, 1889	0:34½
½.	GERALDINE, 4, 122 lbs., at **Morris Park,** Aug. 30th, 1889 . .	0:46
⅝.	BRITANNIC, 5, 122 lbs., at **Morris Park,** Aug. 31st, 1889 . .	0:59
	FORDHAM, 9, 115 lbs., at **Morris Park,** Oct. 4th, 1889	
¾.	EL RIO REY, 2, 126 lbs., at **Morris Park,** Aug. 31st, 1889 . .	1:11
	TIPSTAFF, 3, 107 lbs., at **Morris Park,** Oct. 4th, 1889	
⅞.	BRITANNIC, 5, 110 lbs., at Sheepshead Bay, Sept. 5th, 1889 . . .	1:26⅖
1.	TEN BROECK, 5, 110 lbs., Louisville, May 24th, 1877 (against time)	1:39¾
	MAORI, 4, 105, Chicago (Washington Park), July 12th, 1889 . .	1:39⅘
1 1/16.	WHEELER, T., 3, 98 lbs., St. Louis, June 1st, 1888	1:47¼
	ELYTON, 4, 106 lbs., Chicago (Washington Park), June 28th, 1889	
1⅛.	TERRA COTTA, 4, 124 lbs., Sheepshead Bay, June 23d, 1888 . . .	1:53
1 3/16.	JOE COTTON, 5, 109½ lbs., Sheepshead Bay, Sept. 7th, 1887 . . .	2:00¼
1¼.	KINGSTON, 5, 122 lbs., Brooklyn, Sept. 24th, 1889	2:06½
1 m. 500 yds.	BEND OR, 4, 115 lbs., Saratoga, July 25th, 1882	2:10½
1⅜.	TRIBOULET, 4, 117 lbs., San Francisco (Cal.), April 26th, 1888 .	2:21½
	RICHMOND, 6, 112 lbs., Sheepshead Bay, June 27th, 1888 . . .	
1½.	FIRENZI, 4, 113 lbs., Monmouth Park, Aug. 2d, 1888	2:34
	LUKE BLACKBURN, 3, 102 lbs., Monmouth Park, Aug. 17th, 1880	
	JIM GUEST, 4, 98 lbs., Chicago (Washington Park), July 24, 1886	
1⅝.	HINDOOCRAFT, 3, 75 lbs., **Morris Park,** Aug. 27th, 1889 . . .	2:48
1¾.	GLIDELIA, 5, 116 lbs., Saratoga, Aug. 5th, 1882	3:01
1⅞.	ENIGMA, 4, 90 lbs., Sheepshead Bay, Sept. 15th, 1885	3:20
2.	TEN BROECK, 5, 110 lbs., Louisville, May 29th, 1877	3:27½
2⅛.	MONITOR, 4, 110 lbs., Baltimore, Oct. 20th, 1880	3:44½
2¼.	SPRINGBOK, 5, 114 lbs. / PREAKNESS, a, 114 lbs. — Saratoga, July 29th, 1875	3:56¼
2½.	ARISTIDES, 4, 104 lbs., Lexington, May 13th, 1876	4:27½
2⅝.	TEN BROECK, 4, 104 lbs., Lexington, Sept. 16th, 1876	4:58½
2¾.	HUBBARD, 4, 107 lbs., Saratoga, Aug. 9th, 1873	4:58¾
3.	DRAKE CARTER, 4, 115 lbs., Sheepshead Bay, Sept. 6th, 1884 . .	5:24
4.	TEN BROECK, 4, 104 lbs., Louisville, Sept. 27th, 1876	7:15¾

SOME OF THE LARGEST PAYING $5 MUTUELS.

NICKAJACK (4), at Jerome Park, Oct. 12, 1872 . . . . $1,178 00
WAPAKONITA (3), at Saratoga, July 17, 1882 . . . . 1,080 80
COL. SPRAGUE (5), at Washington, May 18, 1882 . . . . 760 00
HARVARD (3), at Brighton Beach, Aug. 19, 1887 . . . . 760 00
LIMBO (2), 108 lbs., at Sheepshead Bay, Sept. 1, 1888 **(for place)** . 684 80
NATALIE (3), at Brighton Beach, Aug. 16, 1880 . . . . 665 00
HATTIE F. (6), at Baltimore, May 21, 1875 . . . . 648 85
ROY S. CLUKE (4), at Brighton Beach, Sept. 8, 1884 . . . . 622 75
PATROCLES (4), at Washington, May 5, 1887 . . . . 622 25
PHILANDER (3), at Brooklyn, Sept. 18, 1889 . . . . 608 00
JULIET (2), at Chicago (Washington Park), June 30, 1885 . . . . . . 570 00
OSSA (2), at Brighton Beach, Sept. 9, 1889 . . . . 532 00
LEVANT (3), at Latonia, Sept. 22, 1883 . . . . 505 80
KEYSTONE (3), at Brighton Beach, July 4, 1888 . . . . 498 75
FROLIC (4), at Brighton Beach, July 24, 1885 . . . . 445 80
OKOLONA (a), at Brighton Beach, Sept. 1, 1886 . . . . 425 10
TILFORD (4), at Brighton Beach, Nov. 1, 1884 . . . . '. . 422 15
LADY MIDDLETON (4), at Saratoga, Aug. 1, 1879 . . . . 405 60
AURELIUS (6), at Monmouth Park, July 28, 1885 . . . . 403 75
JOE LEWIS (5), at Sheepshead Bay, June 19, 1883 . . . . 403 05
BANDUSIA (2), at Sheepshead Bay, Sept. 6, 1887 . . . . 397 60
EL CAPITAN (4), at Brighton Beach, Nov. 3, 1883 . . . . 385 20
PARKVILLE (4), at Guttenberg, N. J., Nov. 13, 1886 **(for $3.00)** . . 373 35
JESTER (a), at Brighton Beach, Nov. 17, 1886 . . . . 368 10
MACAROON — ENQUIRESS f. (3), at Jerome Park, June 4, 1889 . . . . 356 25
TILFORD (4), at Brighton Beach, Nov. 12, 1884 . . . . 353 45
BILL BRIEN (3), at Brighton Beach, July 12, 1886 . . . . 341 20
SANTA CLAUS (6), at Brighton Beach, Aug. 23, 1886 . . . . 328 70
BASSANIO (3), at Saratoga, Aug. 7, 1886 . . . . 324 60
CHARM (5), at Clifton, N.J., Nov. 3, 1886 . . . . 323 00
FALSEHOOD (4), at Brighton Beach, Aug. 3, 1888 . . . . 322 05
VEXATION (3), at Brighton Beach. Nov. 7, 1882 . . . . 315 85
STANDIFORD KELLER (a), at Brighton Beach, June 3, 1887 . . . . 311 10
SOVEREIGN PAT (3), at Louisville, Oct. 10, 1883 . . . . 312 55
RICO (2), at Brighton, Sept. 15, 1884 . . . . 307 35
KEOKUK (3), at Latonia, May 27, 1885 . . . . 306 35
DAVE S. (5), at Brighton Beach, July 12, 1889 . . . . 306 35
LEROY (4), at Brighton Beach, Sept. 4, 1885 . . . . 300 75
LIZZIE WALTON (4), at Brighton Beach, Aug. 5, 1887 . . . . 300 20
ONEIDA CHIEF (a), at Saratoga, Aug. 4, 1886 . . . . 299 25
ED. BUTTS (4), at Chicago (Washington Park), July 8, 1885 . . . . . 296 80
BADGE (2), at Sheepshead Bay, Sept. 3, 1887 . . . . 295 45
FIREFLY (3), at Jerome Park, May 29, 1888 . . . . 288 60
BRITANNIC (4), at Sheepshead Bay, June 14, 1888 . . . . 287 55
BONNIE S. (4), at Baltimore, May 18, 1886 . . . . 280 25
ADAMANTUS (5), at Rockaway, May 9, 1885 . . . . 279 55
SISTER (2), at Sheepshead Bay, Sept. 1, 1883 . . . . 276 75
JUDGE JACKSON (a), at Lexington, May 7, 1885 . . . . 275 50
LILLIE B. (4), at Brighton Beach, July 18, 1883 . . . . 274 10
GARNET (4), at Brighton Beach, July 29, 1887 . . . . 269 60
THE BOURBON (5), at Washington, April 26, 1888 . . . . 266 00
HOT BOX (3), at Chicago (Washington Park), July 10, 1885 . . . . . 261 25
SUTLER (a), at Brighton Beach, July 21, 1887 . . . . 260 95
SHELBY BARNES (4), at Brighton Beach, Dec. 11, 1884 . . . . 258 85
DAINGERFIELD (5), at Brighton Beach, Sept. 30, 1885 . . . . 248 75